LOVE'S CONFUSIONS

LOVE'S

CONFUSIONS

C. D. C. REEVE

HARVARD UNIVERSITY PRESS
Cambridge, Massachusetts, and London, England
2005

Excerpts from *Poems in English,* by Samuel Beckett, are reprinted by permission of Grove/Atlantic and Calder Publications.

Excerpts from *Collected Poems,* by Philip Larkin, are reprinted by permission of Farrar, Straus and Giroux, LLC, and Faber and Faber Ltd. Copyright © 1988, 1989, by the Estate of Philip Larkin.

Excerpt from *The Keeper of Sheep,* by Fernando Pessoa, is reprinted by permission of the Sheep Meadow Press.

Library of Congress Cataloging-in-Publication Data
Reeve, C. D. C., 1948–
Love's confusions / C. D. C. Reeve.
p. cm.
Includes bibliographical references and index.
ISBN 0-674-01711-0 (alk. paper)
1. Love. I. Title.

BD436.R4 2004
128'.46—dc22   2004054016

For Janet

PREFACE

Like it or not, the stories we tell about love—even the philosophical stories—tend to reveal as much about us as they do about it. For no one can be certain, it seems to me, that he is saying something reasonably public and objective about love, and not erecting a barrier, special to his temperament, against his own personal erotic fears and anxieties. So, though I write in the first person plural, I do so without presumption.

I am a man; my lovers women. So I speak of "our" lovers as shes, not as s/hes. Little would change besides typography, I think, had I inserted the slash mark. I am a man, too, who grew up in Ireland in the Fifties and Sixties, came to the United States in the early Seventies to attend graduate school—and stayed. White, agnostic, deracinated, liberal, financially secure, the loyalties I have are to my friends, and to the world of books and conversations in which I have spent much of my life. All this has surely helped me to see some things about love, but equally surely blinded me to others.

Though the major thematic divisions of my story are revealed in the headings of its ten chapters, a series of overlapping preoccupations crisscrosses them: the influence of Christianity on love, and vice versa; the influence of Platonism on our conceptions of desire and pleasure; the idea of the perfectibility of man and the related idea of Heaven as a place from which pain, suffering, loss, and tragedy are banished; the nature of the self and what love reveals about it. A final preoccupation—exemplified rather than thematized—is with a style of philosophical thinking that is less a matter of analysis and argument than of genealogy, and of situating a target notion within the potentially most revelatory experiential and conceptual field. In the case of love, this field includes infantile experience, sentimentality, work, violence, perversion, and pornography.

I quote and discuss writers of various sorts—philosophers, historians, novelists, poets, psychoanalysts, psychologists, and sociologists—at different junctures. But the engagement is opportunistic and idiosyncratic rather than systematic. We are all amateurs—all *bricoleurs*—when it comes to love. Out of what we chance to love or unlove, or be loved or unloved by, the collage of our love story gets patched together. Among these ingredients will be stories of love itself—stories our culture tells us, stories we learn at our mother's knee. Our own love story resembles, in consequence, a commonplace book—a book, in fact, a bit like this one.

CONTENTS

. . . love's confusions.

—BERTOLT BRECHT, "The Ballad of Sexual Dependency"

A lover never knows what he loves,
Why he loves, or what love is.

—FERNANDO PESSOA, *The Keeper of Sheep*

I

AGAPE, EROS, AND THE WILL

At the center of the Christian message, according to Saint Matthew, lie two great commandments: "Love the Lord your God with all your heart, with all your soul, with all your mind" and "Love your neighbor as yourself."[1] The first initially seems easy to obey. God is a perfect being; none better can be conceived. If love is responsive to value, he must surely attract it. On reflection, though, God's role as enforcer of morals seems to threaten that attraction. It requires him to spy on our secret thoughts and watch us even in our most private moments. And it is hard, isn't it, to love someone so insistently intrusive, so disrespectful of our privacy? It also requires God—as separator of sheep from goats—to punish the wicked. This in itself is not an insuperable obstacle to love, and might even positively inspire it, but it becomes an obstacle when the punishments are infinite and the crimes finite, or when the wicked include those who refuse to love God or who commit sins that may be difficult to understand as wrong (homosexual acts, masturbation). Finally, there is the problem of evil. No need to rehash *this* at any length. God could prevent your innocent baby's agonizing sufferings, yet he doesn't. Love him in the face of that, if you can.

God doesn't watch or punish us or let us suffer for cheap thrills, it might be replied; he does so because he wants what is good for us. And that, some people think, is just what loving someone is. "Loving of any variety," Harry Frankfurt writes, "implies conduct that is designed to be beneficial to the beloved object."[2] Though this may help us see God's apparently unattractive activities as expressions of love—they benefit us in the end—it does so at the cost of making our love for him mysterious. For how can any activity of ours—indeed any activity at all—benefit someone whose very perfection puts him beyond benefit?

God himself does not seem to suppose that to know him is to love him. Why else command our love? But that command too is problematic. For love doesn't seem to be the sort of thing we *can* give on command. We can't love or stop loving because we are told to or because we want or will to. "When it comes to reviving a dying love, what is the good of determination aroused by a sense of duty?"[3] God does not just command us to love, moreover; he commands us to do so with *all* of our heart, soul, and mind. Where, then, we might wonder, will we find the love we need to obey the second commandment? That is Cordelia's question to Lear: "Why have my sisters husbands, if they say they love you all?"[4] Love is *le don de soi*, in any case—the gift of the self. It involves intimacy and the sharing of hearts' secrets. So even if we could love on command or at will, we couldn't love *everybody*. Like socialism, it would take too many evenings.

A solution to these problems is sometimes sought in the actual words Saint Matthew employs. "Agapically love your neighbor as yourself," he says.[5] And agapic love—though something of a blank slate on which we are free to inscribe whatever we wish—is supposed to be different both from erotic love *(eros)* and from friendship *(philia)*. Søren Kierkegaard explains the difference this way. Erotic love and friendship, he says, are mediated by passionate preference. They are spontaneously ignited when they find someone with the right mix of physical, psychological, and spiritual features. They achieve their highest expression, therefore, in the idea that there is only one beloved in the whole world, one person with those features. Agapic love—Christian love—is not like that. It focuses exclusively on spiritual features: "Only in love towards your neighbor is the I that loves defined in purely spiritual terms, and likewise the neighbor."[6] But spiritual features are the same in everyone, since they are features we possess through being reflections—mirrors—of God, made in his image. So when we see each other accurately, rather than through a glass darkly, we are bound—provided we do love God—to love each other too. Love of God and love of our neighbor thus go hand-in-hand. "In love towards the neighbor," Kierkegaard writes, "God is the middle term, so that only by loving God above all else can you love your neighbor in the other man."[7] Whereas erotic love discovers the beloved through being ignited by her, "it is Christian love that discovers and knows that the neighbor exists and, what amounts to the same thing, that everyone is a neighbor."[8]

Because erotic love and friendship are involuntary feelings ignited by the beloved's physical and psychological qualities, they set us no ethical task. We don't have a duty to feel them for anyone and no one has a duty to feel them for us. (That is a prominent part of love's theater, tragic and comic.) Christian love, however, does involve such reciprocal duties. Why? Because it is responsive only to the spiritual features in terms of which the neighbor is defined. "If it weren't a duty to love, the concept of the neighbor wouldn't exist."[9]

But that doesn't help much, does it? It says nothing about why Christian love is less involuntary than erotic love and friendship—it explains only why it's less discriminating. Erotic love is ignited by the pair of laughing blue eyes only you have; Christian love, by the spiritual qualities everyone else has too. Such qualities may be more fundamental to who you are than blue eyes, but the increase in fundamentality seems offset by a decrease in specificity. It isn't you in all your concrete particularity that ignites Christian love, but your spiritual qualities, which are just the image of God reflected in you as in every other person. (Like Rembrandt in his self-portraits, God could appear in different forms in different mirrors, I suppose, but the differences between them would have to be agapically inert. Otherwise, only some people might attract a love that must in fact be indifferently attracted by all.)

Perhaps ignition is the wrong metaphor. Perhaps, as an appreciative response to an autonomous spiritual being, Christian love must itself be somehow autonomous. That would help explain why "in speaking about the first-I or about the alter ego, we do not thereby come a step nearer to the neighbor, since the neighbor is the first-*you*."[10] When I autonomously respond to you as an autonomous spiritual being, I see you not as someone who just happens to have the features needed to play the role of the beloved in *my* love story, but as a coauthor of *our* love story. I see myself in the same way, as someone whose own autonomy is being expressed for yours to respond to.

There is something attractive in this picture. But what such freely given love is and how we freely give it remains mysterious—so mysterious, in fact, that it is tempting to abandon the idea altogether as religious confusion. Alas (or fortunately?), we are in no position to do that, or to sneer at the way Kierkegaard connects love with freedom and moral duty. Marriage vows, in which we promise to love till death parts us, make this plain. So we too seem committed to thinking that love *is* something we can freely give and have a duty to give.

Suppose we are right. Suppose there is a sort of love we can freely and dutifully give. Is it the sort we want to give and get at the altar? We certainly want our new wife to treat us lovingly. If we are a bit strange, we might even want her to love our spiritual self. But there is also something we *do not* want. We do not want her to treat us lovingly out of duty—especially not in bed. Marital love, like gratitude, is a dish we prefer to have served warm—hot even.

If you are like me, in fact, you would rather be loved by someone who treated you badly from time to time than be treated lovingly all the time by someone who didn't love you. Why? Because love leads a lover to do things that nothing else does, like kissing you all over for the sheer pleasure of it, or licking the marmalade from the corners of your mouth, or lighting up when you come into the room, or—more dramatically—taking a bullet for you. No merely Christian lover—however dutiful and committed—could convincingly replicate the actions of a loving heart for long. So there is a tension—maybe an actual contradiction—implicit in our concept of love. We think we can promise love at the altar. Yet we recognize that what we promise there must involve sexual desires and feelings we cannot have at will.

This is to look at the problem from the delivery end. But there is also a problem from the receiving end—a problem Immanuel Kant expresses like this:

> The sexual impulse . . . in and by itself . . . is nothing more than appetite. But, so considered, there lies in this inclination a degradation of man; for as soon as anyone becomes an object of another's appetite, all motives of moral relationship fall away; as object of the other's appetite, that person is in fact a thing, whereby the other's appetite is sated. . . . This is the reason why we are ashamed of possessing such an im-

> pulse, and why all strict moralists, and those
> who wish to be taken for saints, have sought to
> repress and dispense with it. . . . Since the sexual
> impulse is not an inclination that one human
> has for another, qua human, but an inclination
> for their sex, it is therefore a principle of the de-
> basement of humanity.[11]

What we want to give, we may not be able to; what we want to get debases us and turns us into an object.

Either sexual frustration or moral debasement—those are the horns of the dilemma on which love seems to leave us impaled. In Kant's view, however, there is a way between them:

> Marriage signifies a contract between two per-
> sons, in which they mutually accord equal
> rights to one another, and submit to the condi-
> tion that each transfers his whole person en-
> tirely to the other, so that each has a complete
> right to the other's whole person. It is now dis-
> cernible through reason, how sexual intercourse
> may be possible without debasement of human-
> ity or violation of morality. Marriage is thus the
> sole condition for making use of one's sexual
> impulse. If a person now dedicates himself to
> the other, he dedicates not only his sex, but his
> whole person; the two things are inseparable.
> . . . But if I hand over my whole person to the
> other, and thereby obtain the person of the
> other in place of it, I get myself back again, and

have thereby regained possession of myself; for I have given myself to be the other's property, but am in turn taking the other as my property, and thereby regain myself, for I gain the person to whom I gave myself as property. The two persons thus constitute a unity of will. . . . So the sexual impulse creates a union among persons, and only within this union is the use of it possible.[12]

As you can tell, Kant never married and probably never had sex.[13] You have to wonder, even so, at the ease with which he allows debasement to be transformed into a unity of will. You would almost think he had positively warmed to sex, notwithstanding his own moral strictness. Until, that is, you notice the creepily solipsistic nature of the whole transaction. For if what we get when we marry is just what we give, what we get and give must be the same in giver and getter—it must, like Kierkegaard's neighbor, be defined in terms of something akin to spiritual qualities (rational ones, in Kant's view). If I was alone before I gave and got, I seem to be alone afterward too.

"I do not know," Vladimir Nabokov writes, "if it has ever been noted before that one of the main characteristics of life is discreteness. Unless a film of flesh envelops us, we die. Man exists only insofar as he is separated from his surroundings. The cranium is a space-traveller's helmet. Stay inside or you perish. Death is divestment, death is communion. It may be wonderful to mix with the landscape, but to do so is the end of the tender ego."[14] What

goes for tender ego and landscape goes for lover and beloved. Their separateness is a condition of their union—
including their sexual union. Sex with oneself—as we all
know—is a different thing altogether.

Part of what has led Kant astray, I think, is his characterization of the sexual impulse as related not to a person
but to her sex—as if, from the perspective of that impulse,
women are female bodies (or perhaps just vulvas) and all
female bodies the same. But if "the degree and kind of a
person's sexuality reach up into the ultimate pinnacle of
his spirit," as Nietzsche claims,[15] it is also true that what
is at the pinnacle reaches down, as it were, into sexuality's
depths. This female body, like that landscape, unaccount-
ably attracts us. But part of why it—of all similarly config-
ured bodies—does attract us is that it alone is our lover's
and animated by her.

Which isn't to say that we cannot become so obsessed
with our lover's body as to inflict on her—and suffer ourselves—the very kind of degradation Kant imagines. Jôji
Kawai, the narrator of Junichirô Tanizaki's novel *Naomi*,
finds himself in precisely this predicament:

> Whatever transpired in the daytime, I always
> gave into her at night. Or rather than "gave in,"
> I should say that the animal in me was subdued
> by her. The truth is that I still didn't trust her at
> all, but the animal in me forced me to submit
> blindly to her; it led me to abandon everything
> and surrender. Naomi wasn't a priceless trea-
> sure or a cherished idol any more; she'd become

a harlot. Neither lovers' innocence nor conjugal affection survived between us. Such feelings had faded away like an old dream. Why did I feel anything for this faithless, defiled woman? Because I was being dragged along by her physical attractions. This degraded me at the same time as it degraded Naomi, because it meant that I'd abandoned my integrity, fastidiousness, and sincerity as a man, flung away my pride, and bent down before a whore, and I no longer felt any shame for doing so. Indeed, there were times when I worshipped the figure of this despicable slut as though I were revering a goddess.[16]

We readily recognize in Jôji's vivid description an accurate characterization one of sexual desire's liabilities: it can take us over and make us do things of which we are ashamed. But a liability is just that—a liability. Jôji has no more given us a revealing pro-Kant portrait of sexual desire's intrinsic nature or impulse than has Richard von Krafft-Ebing in his *Psychopathia Sexualis.*

What Jôji refers to as "the animal in me" is not the desire of a dog or ape that has somehow ended up controlling him, of course. It is that of a young Japanese man living in Tokyo in the 1920s, whose advanced views are more in his head than in his desires and reactive attitudes. "For me Naomi was the same as a fruit that I'd cultivated myself. I'd labored hard and spared no pains to bring that piece of fruit to its present, magnificent ripeness, and it was only proper that I, the cultivator, should be the one to taste it. No on else had that right. But then, when I wasn't looking, a total stranger had ripped off the skin and taken a bite."[17] Where woman are concerned, we see, Jôji remains a traditional, possessive male. He feels debased by his continued sexual desire for Naomi, not because this desire is naturally debasing, but because of how his social values lead him to represent it to himself, and so to experience it.

In part, no doubt, because she is thirteen years younger than Jôji, and has also been shaped while still an adolescent by his advanced views, Naomi seems somehow aware of all this. Thus, she uses the fact that Jôji desires her in the way he does to teach him to love her as a free and sexually liberated woman. In the end—and despite his feeling that his is now the "subordinate position"—Jôji recognizes that she has succeeded. "If you think my account is foolish," he tells us in the novel's closing paragraphs, "please go ahead and laugh. If you think that there's a moral in it, then, please let it serve as a lesson. For myself, it makes no difference what you think of me; I'm in love with Naomi."[18] When we are considering the liabilities of sexual desire, we should also consider what it can do on behalf of our humanity even when it's misshapen by ideology.

Marriage is an "absolute act," we are told, by which love attempts "to block future time and the possibility of change," and with them "its own diminution and disappearance."[19] Marriage turns love into a "peculiar sentiment that is simultaneously a fatal compulsion and a free choice," an "indissoluble knot that ties together fate and freedom."[20] If the compulsion really is fatal, however, won't it simply reverberate through us, making freedom an illusion? La Bruyère thinks only first love has this involuntary character. "One only loves well once," he writes, "the first time; the loves that follow are less involuntary."[21] It is something, E. M. Forster witheringly comments, that "no one ever said to himself during even his thousandth affair."[22] He is probably right. But in connecting loving well with loving involuntarily, La Bruyère seems right too. "The heart, the heart above all is not free. It is inevitability and the recognition of the inevitable."[23]

Such inevitability occasions anxiety, of course. It makes us feel helpless. Knowing that something is voluntary, however, also causes anxiety: what we can control we can fake. While the inevitability or involuntariness of love may take with one hand, therefore, it partly gives back with the other. We cannot love at will. But we cannot readily fake love either. When the will tries to counterfeit the heart, it is usually detected.

Commitment, like the love that sometimes gives rise to it, can seem to be either an act of will or an involuntary feeling—something given or something drawn forth. In fact, it is probably a little of each. When we take the marriage vows, we typically express already existing feelings of love. At the same time, we voluntarily put a social or religious obstacle in the way of acting on negative feelings. Once married, we have incentives to try to restore or rekindle the loving feelings that time may have eroded—incentives we lacked beforehand. Some of these stem from the marriage contract, others from the products of our initial feelings—a child we both adore, a house we love and can't afford by ourselves, a history and way of life in which we are deeply involved. Anything that weighs against love's enemies helps maintain love. Love may not be directly under our control, but many of the things that help it survive—or perish—are.

Before we fall in love, we know what qualities we are looking for in a lover—or think we do. The profiles on Match .com certainly suggest as much. Once we have fallen in love, it is a different story. When we are pressed to explain why we love our lover, we usually have little to say except what Montaigne says: Because she's she; because I'm me.[24] When it comes to explaining why we love, we are all tongue-tied. We can't capture our lovers with a finite list of qualities for the same reason that we can't replace *Hamlet* with a summary. Loved beings—like great works of art—resist paraphrase. Love, as a result, seems somehow groundless—and so somehow blind.

Still, the illusion that love is grounded in something might not be entirely an illusion. It might simply get things back to front. "God doesn't love that which is already in itself worthy of love," Anders Nygren writes, "but on the contrary, that which in itself has no worth acquires worth just by becoming the object of God's love."[25] Theologically speaking, it is not a compelling idea. God cannot want value-conferring love, since he is already infinitely valuable. So he must want value-responsive love. Apparently, then, value-responsive love is better, since

God surely wants the best. (It noteworthy that we are not commanded to love *God* as we love ourselves.) But that makes God seem a deficient lover—one who loves less well than he wants to be loved.

Where *we* are concerned, on the other hand, value-conferring love might have more promise. We might value where we love, rather than love where we value. That would explain why what we value in our beloved we don't necessarily value in someone else. It would also explain why, when love dies, what we once found beautiful, we may now find commonplace or worse—not even our type, as Swann says of Odette. What we love is well-lit, because love is the source of the light. When the light goes out, the beloved joins the rest of the corps de ballet. Unfortunately, what promises to illuminate love's death darkens its birth. My lover turns my love on. You don't. Love isn't a searchlight. It is more like a security light that only some things trigger. But what things? And why just those? "Attraction is made up of animal humors and spiritual archetypes, of childhood experiences and the phantoms that people our dreams," and so it is "subtle and different in every case."[26]

If the love we give is like that, however, the love we get must be as well. And that renders problematic the commandment to "love your neighbor *as yourself.*" For if we do not know what turns on our love for others, we do not know what turns on our self-love either, and so do not know how to love them as we do ourselves.

2

SEEING, IMPROVISING, AND SELF-LOVE

Kant was well aware that "love as an inclination"—as a feeling or desire—"cannot be commanded." To make sense of the Christian commandments and the marriage vows, therefore, he had to introduce an analogue of Kierkegaard's agape: "beneficence from duty—even though no inclination impels us to it, and, indeed, natural and unconquerable aversion opposes it—is *practical* and not *pathological* love, which lies in the will and not in the propensity of feeling, in principles of action and not in melting sympathy; and it alone can be commanded."[1] The distinction seems inevitable—even if also apparently fatal to our erotic goals. Hot passion is what we want to give and get; cold duty all we can reasonably promise or demand.

Iris Murdoch, however, rejects this dilemma. "I cannot think," she writes, "why Kant, who attributes such majesty to the human soul, should hold that any aversion was strictly 'unconquerable.' Pathological love can be commanded too, and indeed . . . must be commanded."[2] Murdoch's confidence is based on her own interesting conception of pathological love, which she variously describes as "the perception of individuals," "the extremely difficult realization that something other than oneself is real," and "the discovery of reality."[3] What motivates that conception, in turn, is a view about why such perception is difficult: "By opening our eyes we do not necessarily see what confronts us. We are anxiety-ridden animals. Our minds are continually active, fabricating an anxious, usually self-preoccupied, often falsifying veil which partially conceals the world. Our states of consciousness differ in quality, our fantasies and reveries are not trivial and unimportant, they are profoundly connected with our energies and our ability to choose and act. And if quality of consciousness matters, then anything which alters consciousness in the direction of unselfishness, objectivity, and realism is to be connected with virtue."[4] Love, as "the capacity to *see*," is thus what "the liberation of the soul from fantasy" consists in.[5]

In place of the unconquerability of aversion, then, Murdoch offers us the alternative of liberation from self-preoccupied fantasy. But this liberation is not instantaneously available on command: "Moral change and moral achievement are slow; we are not free in the sense of being able suddenly to alter ourselves since we cannot suddenly alter what we can see and ergo what we desire and are compelled by."[6] Nonetheless, it is under our control in the sense that we can work toward it, make progress. Our vital allies in this endeavor are art and morality, which, because they have the same enemies as love, have love as their central organizing concept: "The enemies of art and of morals, the enemies that is of love, are the same: social convention and neurosis. One may fail to see the individual . . . because we are ourselves sunk in a social whole which we allow uncritically to determine our reactions, or because we see each other exclusively as so determined. Or we may fail to see the individual because we are completely enclosed in a fantasy world of our own into which we draw things from outside, not grasping their reality and independence, making them into dream objects of our own. Fantasy, the enemy of art, is the enemy of true imagination: Love, an exercise of true imagination."[7] When we read Tolstoy or Shakespeare—two of Murdoch's favorites—we are shown a world undistorted by self-preoccupied fantasy, with the result that our own vision is helped to become less clouded:

> Good art reveals what we are usually too selfish and too timid to recognize, the minute and absolutely random detail of the world, and reveals it together with a sense of unity and form. This form often seems to us mysterious because it resists the easy patterns of the fantasy, whereas there is nothing mysterious about the forms of bad art since they are the recognizable and familiar rat-runs of selfish day-dream. Good art shows us how difficult it is to be objective by showing us how different the world looks to an

objective vision. We are presented with a truth-
ful vision of the human condition in a form
which can be steadily contemplated. . . . Art
transcends selfish and obsessive limitations of
personality and can enlarge the sensibility of its
consumer. It is a kind of goodness by proxy.
Most of all it exhibits to us the connection, in
human beings, of clear realistic vision with compassion.[8]

Moral change is a process, consequently, of what
Murdoch calls "unselfing," conceived not as a replace-
ment of selfish motives with altruistic or self-sacrificing
ones, but as learning "to keep the attention fixed on the
real situation and to prevent it from returning surrepti-
tiously to the self with consolations of self-pity, resent-
ment, fantasy, and despair."[9] As such it is intrinsically
tied to the Christian virtue of humility. But whereas humility, as an aspect of will, has unattractive connotations
of the doormat, Murdochian humility is something
much more appealing and important—"not a peculiar
habit of self-effacement, rather like having an inaudible
voice," but a "selfless respect for reality and one of the
most difficult and central of all virtues."[10]

About self-preoccupation and its distorting effects on
seeing, Murdoch seems right. Right, too, that overcoming
it through unselfing is typically a slow process art can
further and morality must involve. It isn't just love that
seems more akin to a mode of perception than to a belief
or a desire; other emotions do also. And like the more

familiar sensory modes—smell, taste, vision, touch—they add qualities of their own to the world, qualities into which pain or pleasure are woven (usually in complex and subterranean ways). "If belief maps the world, and desire targets it," as Richard Wollheim puts it, "emotion tints or colors it: it enlivens or darkens it, as the case may be."[11] What seems distinctive about love is that it provides the emotionally colored world with a lighted focus or center, with foreground and background, with depth of field. When the focus is missing we become painfully aware of this. Without our lover in it, the house feels and looks different. Without her to center our vision, other things lose their places, as food so often loses its savor when we eat alone.

Recognizing our lover's central place in our life, and the extent to which our good depends on her, is no easy task. Fantasies of independence fight against our recognition. Yet such recognition does seem more central to love than the desire to confer benefit—an acceptance of our lover's power rather than an expression of our own. Always better lit than everyone else, our lover gives us a new center, outside ourselves, and with it a whole new set of feelings—rage, jealousy, curiosity, envy, hate, suffering, pride, astonishment.

For Kierkegaard, recognizing the reality of other people always leads to love, since what is recognized is the perfect God reflected in them. If what is recognized isn't guaranteed to be perfect, though, it is hard to see how Murdoch can share his confidence. Her love, remember, is "knowledge of the individual," of the real person in all his particularity—something she chastises Kant for being afraid of.[12] But what if the real person is genuinely repellent? May not unconquerable aversion then be the appropriate response, especially for someone who sees him as he really is? "To understand all is to forgive all," it might be replied. But understanding sometimes simply adds contempt to lack of forgiveness.

Murdoch's way of acknowledging this problem is to represent love as imperfectly striving to achieve a goal that is forever beyond it: "Love is the tension between the imperfect soul and the magnetic perfection which is conceived of as lying beyond it. . . . And when we try perfectly to love what is imperfect our love goes to its object via the Good to be thus purified and made unselfish and just."[13] Her major difference with Kierkegaard is just that the Good, rather than being what the beloved reflects, is what measures—and reveals as always imperfect—the lover's own attempts at unselfing.

Witness how a mother, M, trying to see her daughter-in-law, D, in a fairer light is described: "What M is *ex hypothesi* attempting to do is not just to see D accurately but to see her justly or lovingly. . . . M's activity is essentially something progressive, something infinitely perfectible. So . . . M is engaged in an endless task. As soon as we begin to use words such as 'love' and 'justice' in characterising M, we introduce into our whole conceptual picture of her situation the idea of progress, that is the idea of perfection."[14] But this still leaves us in the dark as to why M's increasingly selfless vision won't defeat her love when she sees D as she really is. "In the case of art and nature,"

Murdoch tells us, love as selfless perception "is immediately rewarded by the enjoyment of beauty." "In the case of morality," however, in the case of other people, "although there are sometimes rewards, the idea of reward is out of place."[15] Yet if beloveds are not images of God or the Good, if they are not beautiful, Murdochian love seems as likely to be wrecked by its own success as would its Kierkegaardian analogue in a godless world.

We can also put the problem a different way. Suppose we succeed, as far as a human being can, in seeing Mary, Jane, and Rita in the clear light of Murdoch's love. Why is it only Jane who turns on the security light of our erotic love? Lacking an answer, Murdoch is forced to follow Kant in distinguishing "the highest love" from erotic love: "I have not spoken of the role of love in its everyday manifestations. . . . One cannot but agree that in some sense this is the most important thing of all; and yet human love is normally too profoundly possessive and also too 'mechanical' to be a place of vision. There is a paradox here about the nature of love itself."[16]

Indeed, there is.

Like the narrator of J. M. Coetzee's memoir, *Youth,* even unprepossessing people are attracted to the idea that love can discover value where nothing else can: "There is something essential he lacks, some definition of feature. Something of the baby still lingers in him. How long before he will cease to be a baby? What will cure him of babyhood, make him into a man? What will cure him, if it were to arrive, is love. He may not believe in God but he does believe in love and the power of love. The beloved, the destined one, will see at once through the odd and even dull exterior he presents to the fire that burns within him. Meanwhile, being dull and odd looking are part of a purgatory he must pass through in order to emerge, one day, into the light: the light of love."[17] Murdoch and Kierkegaard are brought close in this passage. Unless we can be confident a fire has been kindled in us, how can we be confident there is one there for love to find?

But need it be *a fire* love finds? "Those of us who seem immodestly accurate transcriptions of a dream" may, as Philip Larkin writes, love and mate only with "an equal candescence." "Adder-faced singularity," on the other hand, or "skin disease," may be less discriminating. "A nailed-up childhood" or "soft horror of living" may do for them. Ugly may find ugly, as beauty beauty, and so all are "gathered in," none "wasted."[18] Alternatively, love may find beauty where nonlove would not. "Now and then," Charles Baxter tells us in his novel *Saul and Patsy,* Delia's husband, Norman, "would rub his scalp, for example, then examine his fingertips for dandruff, and if there happened to be any dandruff there near the fingertips, he would, if he thought no one was watching, slyly slip the fingertips close to his nose, for a smell." Not an attractive habit. But Delia, picturing it after Norman's death, "felt tender toward it, and him. It pierced her. The gesture made her see the child in him, which, all day long, he was at pains to conceal."[19]

"Far more mysterious than the call of sex to sex," E. M. Forster writes, "is the tenderness that we throw into that call."[20] It is revelatory, all the same, that what evokes tenderness in Delia, as so often in ourselves, is precisely the child in her lover, with his innocent curiosity about his body and its products. That is one reason we are lucky to have been—and in various ways to remain—children. When the child is glimpsed, the concealing adult may be bathed for a moment in his charm.

Being nonspiritual, nonrational, and not necessarily beautiful, however, the child isn't particularly well-suited to work his magic on the eye of morally serious Kierkegaardian or Murdochian love. Yet the tender eye he does charm is one that, in love, we want to find. "For man," writes Proust, "is that ageless creature who has the faculty of becoming many years younger in a few seconds, and who, surrounded by the walls of the time through which he has lived, floats within them as in a pool the surface level of which is constantly changing so as to bring him within range now of one epoch now of another."[21] When the surface level brings us within the range of childhood, we need to be tenderly babied again and aimlessly played with. And who, if not a lover, can satisfy that need? To whom else, indeed, would we willingly reveal it?

The desire to be seen—known—may seem an undemanding one. But "getting people right is not what living is all about. . . . It is getting them wrong that is living, getting them wrong and wrong and wrong and then, on careful consideration, getting them wrong again. That is how we know we are alive: we are wrong."[22] You don't have to have tried psychoanalysis to recognize the truth in this. "Only galley slaves know themselves," Nietzsche says, expressing a similar thought in a characteristically more offensive—and more challenging—way.[23] Yet the idea of being known remains perennially attractive. The *pour-soi,* as Jean-Paul Sartre says, longs for the self-identity of the *en-soi.* We want to be things. We want to rest secure in what we are, helpless but excused—or be held there. Christianity acknowledges this wish and—disastrously—grants it: "Now we see only puzzling reflections in a mirror," Saint Paul tells us in his well-known discussion of love. "But then we shall see face to face. My knowledge now is partial; then it will be whole, like God's knowledge of me."[24] When we are seen in that all-revealing light, what we experience will be not love, I think, but crystallization—suspended animation.

Murdoch describes the lover's task as infinite, implying that it can never be finished. She also speaks of it as progressive, as approaching—if never reaching—perfection. Her image of love is thus Saint Paul's made immanent and asymptotic. It shares the idea that in someone's mind, at least, whether God's or our lover's, we can be as we really are. But that isn't love so much as the inverse of a possessive fantasy. It isn't what we really want—not even as an unachievable ideal.

While Murdoch's lover has work to do, unselfing and seeing, her beloved seems to sit passively waiting to be gazed at. But being able to accept love—being able to lower our defenses in the face of it—is just as active a thing as loving, just as much a part of love. Love, when *we* feel it, "disarms our emotional defenses; it makes us vulnerable to the other."[25] Love, when someone else feels it for us, is an invitation to disarm that may simply make us anxious, more defensive. Goethe notwithstanding, if I love you, it *is* your business.[26] Passivity, in fact, is typically an achievement, like standing perfectly still. To succeed it must be keyed to the invitation to activity it aims to resist.

It might be something about me in particular that arouses your anxiety, that makes you not want me to love and see you. Yet it might not be up to you. You might want to let me love you, but find you can't. Your defenses aren't under your control. Alternatively, your defenses might be your way of flirting or of heightening tension: "no" means no—except when it means try harder or another time. Or they might be part of your manner—as they are for Dr. Balbi in Anita Brookner's *Bay of Angels*. "Behind his professional reserve," Zoë Cunningham says of him, "lay vast areas of personal reserve which had to be protected at all costs. By nature laconic and sceptical he preferred to be seen as formidable, unapproachable, perhaps unaware that such a stance was an open invitation to marauders. . . . His was the only narrative I now cared to follow, though he managed to make it as opaque, as uninteresting, as possible. I admired the technique, having been unable to acquire it myself. It is a defensive strategy; the object is to make the terrain safe from invasion."[27] Like a novelist who writes in a style that will keep the interest of only her sorts of readers, Balbi has developed a defense only his sort of woman can breach.

And Zoë turns out to have what it takes—tact, discretion, clearsightedness.

Love is an active and interactive process, a drama in which even Murdoch-style seeing is two-sided, not one-sided. The unmistakable look of love—the look the Madonna has in so many Renaissance paintings as she gazes at the infant Jesus—has a story in it, a promise. In the case of the Madonna, the story of Christ's future Passion and death. That story was fated, of course, foretold, fore-ordained. Ours is more often improvisational. We make it up as we go along, even if never entirely from whole cloth.

The drama of intimate life is a drama of disclosure, of revealing what is there. It is also a drama of transformation, in which what is revealed is changed, and ourselves with it. For instance, most people know the feeling of being silenced. We are trying to express our feelings—feelings that are inchoate and fragile, feelings of which we are unsure or even ashamed. And our lover doesn't help them find a voice. She doesn't respond in a way that leads forward. Such feelings are like embryos. In a bad relationship, they get stunted, deformed, bottled up, condemned to boring repetition. In a good one, they get elaborated and refined—they get to develop, grow. They become what they are in part through getting worked out in the emerging plot we improvise with our lover (though not, naturally, just with her). We keep having to reabsorb them as she reflects them back to us. They are what they become in the to-and-fro. Like anything with a history, they have no fixed essence. They might grow into one thing or into something else altogether.

"I'm talking about recognizing," as Philip Roth puts it, "that one is acutely a performer, rather than swallowing whole the guise of naturalness and pretending that it isn't a performance but you. All I can tell you with certainty is that I . . . have no self independent of my imposturing, artistic efforts to have one. . . . I am a theater and nothing more than a theater."[28] True, Roth does acknowledge a minimal natural self, a "root of all impersonation." But that acknowledgment doesn't go far enough. Not every impersonation is in every natural self's range, anymore than it is in every actor's. The very notion of range, indeed, makes plain our need to recognize something that determines it. You have your root, I mine, and they are intimately our own. All the same, the idea of the self as a theater does capture an important truth. We aren't still-lives waiting to attract a lover with our static beauty. We are actors playing roles for actors playing roles for us, each adapting himself to the other who is adapting herself to him. And as habits congeal into second nature, so role congeals into self. At fifty, our face—whether deserved or not—has become the mask that love (among other things) has made of it.

"What we think of as 'mind,'" according to the novelist William Gibson, "is only a sort of jumped-up gland, piggybacking on the reptilian brain stem and the older, mammalian mind . . . [which] spreads continent-wide beneath it, mute and muscular, attending its ancient agenda."[29] We have an instinctual nature and a psychic nature whose aims do not always coincide: we can commit suicide to achieve our goals. But in the beginning, at least, our instinct for self-preservation is no doubt supreme. To the extent that it counts as a primitive form of self-love, therefore, self-love *is* bound to exist in all of us—as Saint Matthew, in common with many others, presupposes.

Much on Gibson's agenda was inscribed there in the so-called circumstances of evolution millennia ago. Yet it continues to operate on us, as on other animals—although not always in transparent ways. Evolutionary psychologists tell us, for instance, that women have an instinctual (or genetic) propensity to select a nonpromiscuous male (a so-called dad) as a husband, but a promiscuous one (a so-called cad) as biological father for their children.[30] That way, the theory goes, more copies of their genes will make it into the future. Unless the women are quite eccentric, however, their motive for being unfaithful won't be to serve their genes. Instincts register in our conscious minds in ways that often conceal their true nature, appearing there as desires whose content bears little obvious relation to what the instinct itself serves to promote. (Which isn't to say that we couldn't come to know their true nature, or, having come to know, that we couldn't set about trying to amend. Biology isn't fate.)

Huge changes occur as a result of socialization—a process which begins on the first day of life (if not before) and which "culminates in the social individual, a speaking entity that has an identity and a social state, conforms more or less to certain rules, pursues certain ends, accepts certain values, and acts according to motivations and ways of doing things that are sufficiently stable for its behavior to be, most of the time, foreseeable . . . for other individuals."[31] This new social self is the successor of the presocial—and somewhat vestigial—one we love and preserve instinctually. And what is remarkable about it—among other things—is that it involves all sorts of negative or hostile attitudes toward its predecessor. Once socialized, I am bound to be disgusted by some of my instinctual urges—like Norman's to smell the dandruff under his fingernails. That is part of the point of socialization.

The social individual is largely, if not entirely, the result of the intentional actions of *other people.* But once we have acquired the capacity to reflect on ourselves and have gained some small measure of independence, we can begin to shape ourselves. The *mature self* we get then, as the product of our own activities and the expression of our own values, may seem better suited to attract our love than either of its predecessors. Yet that self, too, may fail to win our love. In part, this may be because of what the mature self inherits ineluctably from the social self: in a racist, homophobic, capitalistic society, a poor, black, homosexual will have a hard time loving even the mature self he has helped shape, and wants—and wants to want—to have. Even when the social self is absorbed into the mature one without setting off any negative feelings, however, love for it may be weakened or missing altogether.

Forster's Mr. Fielding, in *A Passage to India,* is an example. In the following scene, having just resigned from the

Anglo-Indian Chadrapore Club, he is standing on its balcony and taking his leave:

> It was the last moment of the light, and as he gazed at the Marabar Hills they seemed to move graciously towards him like a queen, and their charm became the sky's. At the moment they vanished they were everywhere, the cool benediction of the night descended, the stars sparkled, and the whole universe was a hill. Lovely, exquisite moment—but passing the Englishman with averted face and on swift wings. He experienced nothing himself; it was as if someone had told him there was such a moment, and he was obliged to believe. And he felt dubious and discontented suddenly, and wondered whether he was really and truly successful as a human being. After forty years' experience, he had learned to manage his life and make the best of it on advanced European lines, had developed his personality, explored his limitations, controlled his passions—and he had done it all without becoming either pedantic or worldly. A creditable achievement, but as the moment passed he felt he ought to have been working at something else the whole time—he didn't know at what, never would know, never could know, and that was why he felt sad.[32]

The exquisite sunset moment is experienced as if by hearsay, filtered through the structure of the self Mr. Fielding has helped to produce. Yet it is enough, even in such muted form, to make him doubt the person he has become. The unknown, never-to-be-known self flickers before him as a self he might have loved with greater joy.

Mr. Fielding has built his mature self, Forster shows us, too much under the influence of anxieties about life management, too much insulated from the sort of experience that briefly discontents him with himself. Louis, the narrator in François Mauriac's *Knot of Vipers,* has arrived at his much greater discontent—amounting to actual self-hatred—by a different and more traumatic route. He is talking in bed with his young bride when she tells him about someone she had been in love with earlier. Another man might have taken this confession in stride. But Louis has doubts, stemming from his early socialization, about whether he is worthy of love. So he takes his wife to be "revelling in a delicious memory," when she is really just being intimate, revealing her heart.[33] He decides that she married him only because her love affair had made her unlikely to find a husband of her own social class. In agony, he tries to handle his pain through "a frenzied attempt to stifle his young love."[34] The negative feelings marshaled and nurtured to do the stifling are the book's eponymous knot of vipers, which hold him in their grip without really being connected to his core self. "All my life long," he tells us, "I have been a prisoner of a passion which never really possessed me."[35] It is only when his wife dies and his own death approaches that he sees what this has done to him. "Everything in me, even my voice, even my gestures, belongs to the monster whom I reared against the world, the monster to whom I gave my name."[36]

Louis and Fielding are hardly extreme cases. "When our mission is to find our core self," the social critic William Ian Miller writes, "we know we are in its near environs when our consciousness of it sets off unpleasant feelings of shame, self-doubt, and suspicion."[37] It is often what we can least stand about ourselves that we—despite our self-transformative activities—seem most to be.

When we think of loving others, we are drawn, as Iris Murdoch is, toward thoughts of identifying them, seeing them as they really are. But while loving others seems hindered by how little we know about them, self-love seems hindered by how much we know. Others see some of our actions; we see all of them—and our intentions, thoughts, feelings, and fantasies as well. Hence the apparently self-revelatory character of self-disgust and self-hatred. They seem too damning a response to the core self to be anything but authentic.

Yet, as revelatory as self-disgust and self-hatred can be, they are no more so than the very different emotions characteristic of self-transcendence, of absorption in something or someone besides ourselves. What we can lose ourselves in shows as much about who we are as what we can't stand being. "Towards the outside," Freud tells us, "the ego seems to maintain clear and sharp lines of demarcation. There is only one state . . . in which it does not do this. At the height of being in love the boundary between ego and object threatens to melt away. Against all the evidence of his senses, a man who is in love declares that 'I' and 'you' are one, and is prepared to be-have as if it were a fact."[38] By analogy with interpersonal love, self-love might then seem not so much a matter of seeing or knowing as a matter of becoming one with one-self, of having inner boundaries melt away.

Again, the case of interpersonal love helps to show more concretely what such melting of boundaries might actually involve. "Being femme for me," Mykel Johnston says, "is linked to my treasuring of butch women, to my deep erotic need and hunger for the qualities that have banished them. To be femme is to give honor where there has been shame."[39] Initially, Johnston's lover is ashamed of her own sexual qualities and desires. When she sees that Johnston cherishes, honors, and erotically needs them, however, her attitude is potentially changed. If she wants Johnston's love, they become qualities and desires she needs to value, enhance, and develop. As a result, the boundary shame has erected between those qualities and herself has become exposed to a psychological force with the potential to melt it somewhat.

We sometimes say that part of why we love another per-son is that we love who we are with her. She makes us feel good about ourselves. This may be because she encour-ages us to play a role in which qualities we already love in ourselves are highlighted, and others we dislike are backgrounded. But it may also be because she finds value where we previously found only its opposite. She brings out something new in us for us to love. We need not im-mediately share her evaluation of it, but to the extent that we want to be loved by her, we have a strong incentive to do so. This, after all, is just the good version of a process that in its bad version is all too familiar: trying against the grain of ourselves to become what our lover wants.

In losing ourselves in what we love, whether a person or an activity, we find in it a self we love. So even if there is much in us that we may never be able either to love or modify, in loving something else, we may become so absorbed as to forget or overlook what we cannot change. In the end, if we are lucky, the unloved qualities either atrophy, or become perfecting flaws, or simply disappear in the larger pattern that practice has made strong. *If* we are lucky.

"The individual," according to Alexander Herzen, "posits himself as his own end. Society posits itself in the same way. These kinds of antinomies . . . constitute the poles of everything alive: they are insoluble because in effect their resolution would be the indifference of death, the equilibrium of rest, whereas life exists only in movement: with the total victory of the individual or of society, history would end with predatory individuals, or with a peacefully grazing herd."[40] Inside the individual, too, there are equivalent antinomies. What ensures our psychological equilibrium—for example, by insulating us from threatening experiences—is the enemy of what promotes needed psychological change. It is better, therefore, not to fetishize the *unity* of the self, especially if this is conceived in overly rigid terms. The love that melts bad boundaries to produce desirable change must also help sustain good ones required for no less desirable equilibrium.

A flexible self, able to handle change without losing equilibrium, will no doubt often find exits in what seem like no-exit situations, re-railing a life or love that seems derailed. But no self, however resourceful, can manage this task indefinitely. Reality is too complex and in too much flux for that. Wars break out. Illnesses strike. Lovers die. Anxieties overpower defenses. The world that once helped make sense of our lives disappears. But then, we don't last forever either, and so we don't need the resources that forever would require.

3

FIRST LOVE AND AFTER

I see you—*you*—and, whether I want to or not, I get turned on, hooked. For Saint Augustine, such involuntary responsiveness is a defect, a punishment. Before Adam ate the apple, he had voluntary control of his erections and Eve (presumably) of her wetness. Afterward, it was a different story: voluntary control was lost, but longed for. That is why a true "friend of wisdom" would choose to beget children without orgasm, since, when "the emotion of the mind is united with the craving of the flesh, it convulses the whole man, so that there follows a pleasure greater than any other: a bodily pleasure so great that, at that moment of time when he achieves his climax, the alertness and, so to speak, vigilance of a man's mind is almost entirely overwhelmed."[1] No sexual pleasure for the wise, then, and no cold beer either—at least not very much. Rational control is too precious to give up even for an ecstatic moment.

Augustine envies Adam and Eve. Homer—rightly, in my view—is more circumspect. Despite the disaster involuntary sexual desire brought on the Greeks and Trojans, he does not think we should seek to extirpate it. When Hector is berating Paris for the troubles he has brought on the Trojans, the issue is explicit:

> No, don't stand up to Menelaus, you might find out
> What kind of a man it is whose wife you're sleeping with.
> You think your lyre will help you, or Aphrodite's gifts,
> Your hair, your pretty face, when you sprawl in the dust?

A devastating criticism. But it is to Paris that Homer awards the yet more devastating reply:

> That is only just, Hector. You've got a mind
> Like an axe, you know, always sharp,
> Making the skilled cut through a ship's beam,
> Multiplying force—nothing ever turns your edge.
> But don't throw golden Aphrodite's gifts in my face.
> We don't get to choose what the gods give us, you know,
> And we cannot toss their gifts aside.[2]

Like Aphrodite's gifts, many other valuable things enter the world independently of will and reflection and might not exist or survive if these had greater scope or power than they do. Love often begins in the sheer accident of sexual responsiveness—or in the mysterious psychobiology of the desire for children. Would it still begin if they were taken away or made subject to rational reflection and control? It is in the nature of the case that we cannot be sure.

Sexual desire isn't just involuntary, moreover; it is

opaque—responsive and inciting to strange things. Some of these, like kissing, are no less so for being familiar: "Ravished over her I lay, full lips full open, kissed her mouth. Yum. Softly she gave me in my mouth the seedcake warm and chewed. Mawkish pulp her mouth had mumbled sweet and sour with spittle. Joy: I ate it: joy. Young life, her lips that gave me pouting. Soft, warm, sticky gumjelly lips."[3] Joy, indeed! But strange joy.

Other things love incites are stranger still—so strange, in fact, so potentially alien to our own erotic repertoire, that they may cause us positive disgust:

> A boy, twentyish, very skateboard, comes on the low stage at one end of the bar, wearing lycra shorts and a dog collar. He sits loosely in a restraining chair. His partner comes out and tilts the bottom's head up to the ceiling, stretching out his throat. Behind them is an array of foods. The top begins pouring milk down the boy's throat, then food, then more milk. It spills over, down his chest and onto the floor. A dynamic is established between them in which they carefully keep at the threshold of gagging. The bottom struggles to keep taking in more than he really can. The top is careful to give him just enough to stretch his capacities. From time to time a baby bottle is offered as respite, but soon the rhythm intensifies. The boy's stomach is beginning to rise and pulse, almost convulsively. . . . Finally, . . . the top inserts two, then three fingers in the bottom's throat, insistently

offering his own stomach for the repeated climaxes.[4]

Sex can lead a lover to want to do such things. And if we don't want to do them, it can lead her to try to get us to want to, to turn us on to what turns her on. And if she can't, it can lead her to abandon us for someone else. It isn't always easy to understand such wants or their peculiar importance and insistence. But sometimes in love—as in life more generally—we have to accept things we don't understand. Tolerating the tolerable is easy. It is what we find intolerable that tests our tolerance.

Encountering the opaque in our sexual desires or in those of our lover lends credibility to psychoanalysis, I think, and to its accounts of love and of the self that wants to give and get it. For whatever else it does or claims to do, psychoanalysis provides "a rich fund of theoretical and conceptual resources for the creation of a reflexively ordered narrative of self," a way of bringing the "past 'into line' with the exigencies of the present" that helps makes the opacity of our desires somewhat more intelligible.[5] In this way of thinking of it, psychoanalysis enters our love stories not primarily as a science or branch of medicine but as something hermeneutic— something that helps us make sense of our experience and "find new things about ourselves that we didn't know we could value."[6]

When a very young child is hungry, it is as if he is trying to feel the temperature of something too hot to touch:

what he feels isn't the temperature, but a pain that hides or occludes it. He can't experience the hunger, because he is so overwhelmed. All he can do is scream out the pain or anxiety it causes. But if he has a good enough mother, she can help him experience it. When he screams it out, she understands and comforts and feeds him. She returns his hunger to him as something he can tolerate and experience: "See, it isn't so terrible. Mommy can make it go away."

First love, as opposed to what is conventionally so called, is the love expressed in this story—the one that begins with our mother, with her look, smell, sound, taste, and touch. True, she may not have been very loving. But if she hadn't been minimally so, we wouldn't be here. If someone hadn't taken care of us and satisfied our basic infantile needs, we would be dead. And taking care of someone—just because he needs it—is often an act of love.

When he is around six months old, a child sees his image in a mirror.[7] He feels the pertinence or salience of what he sees in a new way. He smiles hesitantly and looks to his mother for corroboration, as if to say, "Is that . . . ?" She returns his smile: "Yes, that's *you!* Aren't you a handsome baby?" And it is his mother's love and approval of his image that attaches it to him, that gives it to him as something he wants to be—a sort of embryonic self, whose outline serves as the boundary of what is him and what isn't. His hunger goes inside that boundary. Her love goes inside the boundary of an image, *inner-Mommy,* that bears the same relation to her as his image bears to him.

If love for him—or for his self-image—stays securely inside inner-Mommy, the result is pleasure. But if his mother is actively disapproving or punitive, the resultant pain may threaten to drive out the love. Then a new image, a "bad" inner-Mommy, may appear to contain the disapproval, leaving the love securely in the "good" mother. This eases the difficulty and restores the pleasure. A structure of interrelated inner objects or inner figures emerges as this process continues and develops.[8]

The mirror story is an aid to the imagination: children had egos long before there were actual mirrors. Still, the ego derives from something like a mirror image—"from bodily sensations, chiefly from those springing from the surface of the body."[9] Since that surface, in addition to being visible, is sensitive to pleasure, pain, and many other things, the ego is complex, multi-sense. It derives from being stroked and bathed, from seeing spontaneous gestures and expressions reflected in the mother's face ("the precursor of the mirror," as Winnicott calls it), from feeling skin in contact with clothes, as well as from visual, olfactory, and other stimuli.[10] The result is an infantile self-image with an inside and outside that are not solely visual. That is why love—something not merely visual—can be represented as inside it.

Sucking on a mother's nipple leads to pleasure. It gets certain neurons to fire. Then sucking on a thumb gets them to fire. Then the child learns to get them to fire without sucking. The skill needed to make them fire has been internalized. Now he can please himself by fantasy sucking—something multi-sense imagery is typically exploited to facilitate. But to be able to fantasize about himself or his Mommy, or about his Mommy doing things to him, requires more skills than those involved in mere internalization.

As adults, we actively produce some of our thoughts. Yet the vast majority of them just drift in and out of our minds, more or less randomly. Except for the obsessive ones. No matter how hard we try to push them away, they keep forcing their way back in. Or those—like people's names, or the memories of unbearably traumatic experiences—that flit away when we try to focus on them. The helplessness we feel in such cases, the child feels more generally. But when he acquires the ability to push something out of his body or suck it in, he begins to feel less helpless. As he learns to internalize these abilities, he becomes able to push the corresponding multi-sense image out of his self-image or keep it within it. That is to say, he becomes able to *fantasize* doing these things. His mind or self is no longer a place where desires simply occur, but one where active desiring—desiring that manifests a developing competence or ability to desire—happens. The pleasure or pain he gets from sucking something into his skin envelope or expelling it from there, he can get from fantasizing doing so. Such fantasizing is infantile thinking. The multi-sense images or inner figures it utilizes— embryos that will develop into fully fledged concepts—are its tools.

Things are sucked into the child's body through his mouth and pushed out through his anus and urethra. These comings and goings stimulate nerve endings, create neural pathways, develop muscle memory, and make these openings increasingly sensitive, increasingly perceptive: they enmind the body, embody the mind. When the child is hungry, he gets pleasure from the nipple entering his mouth, from the warm milk filling it and flowing down his gullet into his stomach, where it vanquishes the tormenting hunger pains. But if Mommy misinterprets his cries of distress as cries of hunger and forces her nipple into his mouth, the very same things are painful and he tries to resist. He might regurgitate the milk, force it back out again. The same sort of thing happens on the other end. A lump of stool lodged in his intestines feels uncomfortable, like something inside trying to hurt him. As it moves down into his rectum, it feels rasping and scraping. As it leaves his body it stretches and burns his anus. In the diaper, it irritates his sensitive skin.

These dramas of eating and excreting, and the fantasies associated with them, all involve Mommy, or some equivalent caregiver. She is the one who interprets what is happening and replaces pain with pleasure, if she interprets correctly. In the process, she provides her child with an embryonic model of loving relationships, a foundation for the concept of love he will have as an adult. It is partly for this reason that when in later life he finds someone or something else to love, his finding "is in fact a refinding"—a partial recapitulation of his infantile experience, rather than the utterly opaque mystery it may seem to him to be.[11]

Because he is a little animal, a product of chance and necessity, the model Mommy provides includes putting stuff in his mouth, cleaning his bottom, taking away his pee and poop. Strange things to be parts of a model of love. Until, that is, you look at what lovers do. The mouth, the nipples, the anus, the urethra are all important characters in the theater of Eros—as, for that matter, are food and drink, shit and piss. The child's early lessons in love explain why. If our mouths weren't at one end of our intestines and our anuses at the other, our love lives would be very different.

Because the child's relationship with Mommy is his model for understanding his relationship with other things, he tends to personify them—including those that he imagines competing with him for her love. Since Daddy—if there is an actual Daddy around—is one of those things, the embryonic concept corresponding to him is *inner-Daddy*. But in a world where Mommy stays at home and Daddy goes out to work, Daddy *is* intelligibly thought of as "the prime representative of the outside world," since he is the one on whom it particularly impinges.[12] As a result, the embryonic concept of reality is functionally equivalent to inner-Daddy. It is Daddy in particular, then, that a child experiences as cutting him off from pleasure—as castrating him, to put it tendentiously—by preventing him from spending all his time with his Mommy. But if Daddy is missing, some other aspect of reality—such as work and Mommy's need to return to it—may have the same effect.

The child's fear of being cut off from pleasure gives the inner-Daddy, the internalized representative of reality (including moral reality), a lot of power. In the guise of the superego, the inner-Daddy opposes the various desires for pleasure contained in the instinctual id, and leads to their repression. Instead of being accessible on the inside, they become things the child cannot bear to have even there.

The enormous power the child has in his own fantasies—where there are no obstacles at all to his getting what he wants—conflicts with his developing experience of reality. He sees that Daddy is big and strong, whereas he is small and weak. Whatever he can do to love Mommy, Daddy must be able to do so much more. And it is this realization, which turns the superego into an object of aspiration as well as of fear, that reveals Daddy as someone he wants to be or be like, as someone he—ambivalently—loves.

This simplified Freud-inspired story is male-focused and psychological. It has an easily overlooked sociohistorical dimension, however, which explains why its extension to girls and women proved problematic. In Freud's social world, men's sexual desires were treated as known quantities. But "an average uncultivated woman" had the polymorphous perverse sexual predisposition of a child. Led on by "a clever seducer," she was supposed to find "every sort of perversion to her taste," and to "retain them as part of her own sexual activities."[13] In other words, she was a sexual blank slate on which men wrote their own sexual wishes, so that hers became an unfathomable mystery: "The great question that has never been answered, and which I have not yet been able to answer, despite my thirty years of research into the feminine soul, is 'What does a woman want?'"[14]

Had Freud been analyzing men brought up in a society

dominated by women, he would probably have found them equally sexually mysterious, since reality would have entered their lives pretty much as it in fact entered those of the women he analyzed. "Digital orgasms"—orgasms mythically produced in fingers when they stimulate clitorises—might then have left men's sexual wishes as opaque as vaginal orgasms in fact left women's.[15]

Nonetheless, when suitably modified, psychoanalysis gives us a way of thinking about the infantile mind— whether male or female—that allows us to make sense of the idea of infantile love, and so of some of the mysteries adult love inherits from it.

Fully fledged thinking is propositional. It is thinking *that* the world is some way—that the sun is shining, that the moon is a balloon. But the idea that only propositional thinking is genuine thinking is as much a prejudice as the idea that only genital sex is sex. Infantile thoughts are embryonic, and so, like infantile sexuality, foreign to us. They may not be propositional, but they do have content—even if it isn't content that can be readily captured in adult conceptual terms.

Infantile thinking is modeled in part on ingestion and excretion, on taking in and pushing out. Like dreaming, which it resembles, it isn't logical, causal, or subject-predicate in form. Yet a capacity for adult thought presupposes a capacity for infantile thought. If we can't learn to keep things in mind instead of immediately pushing them out, we can't learn to experience the world or think reality-related thoughts. Various mental illnesses reveal as much. The agoraphobic can't think about the empty space that faces him, and so can't say what it is he fears.

In order for us to learn, the world has to capture and hold our attention. It has to "present itself to us as worthy of our love."[16] Computers aren't like that. They aren't libidinal. They don't get turned on—except literally—or get bored and start fantasizing. That may be one reason we are reluctant to believe they really think. We dimly intuit that thinking, too, is a libidinal activity.

A child can't feed himself. What he needs isn't simply food, but *to be fed*—to be part of a drama, a game. Mommy doesn't so much present him with an object of thought or attention, as coax him into playing a role in a drama involving food—a drama that interests him because of need. Then, as he matures, he gets involved in more and more of the drama, more and more of the game. Until finally—if all goes well—he becomes a player in the game of life.

Dramas and games are often contrasted with reality. "No game-players," the personal ads say. But if you include yourself and others in reality, all the world really is a stage. We are handed a part in a play already in progress and we have to muddle through somehow. The baby, the schoolboy, the soldier, the old man dying—lots of life is like that. We get to improvise a bit. But we don't make up the whole thing from scratch. It is there—the play, reality—and we have to accommodate ourselves to it as best we can.

Initially, this accommodation involves acquiring the

ability to control our wishes and inner objects. But the game we learn to play with them is still subject to something like the pleasure principle. We fantasize about getting rid of Daddy (reality), so we can have Mommy's love for ourselves. But for all we do, there Daddy still is. And it is his wish that proves more effective. He interrupts the fantasy we have of being Mommy's only love: "Time for bed now, sonny Jim." As we learn the pleasure game, then, we are also learning the reality game. If our fantasies were omnipotent, reality would conform to them. Since they aren't, when we try to act them out—when we try to play baby the way we play inner-baby—we suffer the pains of frustration. Daddy prevents us from doing what we want to do.

In that way, as in others, reality breaks into the inner world. Then, for all the skill we have developed, we can't keep the pain levels down by manipulating inner objects. It is as if they take on a life of their own. They refuse to obey us, no matter how skillful we become. Which is just as well. If reality didn't break in, we would have no incentive to leave the world of fantasy for the vastly richer one of reality. Not that we ever do fully leave it.

In school, my friends and I developed a code to use among ourselves in which English words were assigned nonstandard meanings. "Book" meant "teacher," for example. The problem was that we kept treating these words as if they had their usual meanings. It is amazing how difficult it was not to do so. Similarly, the child has his inner figures. He used to play fantasy with them. But now he has to play reality with them as well. That is like trying to play code with English words. So just as we were always in danger of slipping from code into English, a child is always in danger of slipping from reality into fantasy, always in danger of acting out—a danger he learns to minimize, if he does, by playing a lot more reality with other children. He learns to be a grown-up by playing at being one.

Similarly with thinking. A child learns to play at it in part by learning how to move his body appropriately, as he learned to control his anal sphincter, and so to move his thoughts as well. As he begins to come to terms with reality, one set of skills and habits gets layered on top of another, until eventually it becomes more second nature than the first. He learns not to be distracted by his own wishes into shifting his attention away from the game. The same is true of adult thoughts. They, too, develop out of—and never completely leave behind—the sort of wishes and wish-infused perceptions of childhood.

That is surely one reason lovers tend to see not the real person in front of them, but the perfect lover of their fantasy—someone who is partly a product of their own past experience of love. Seeing what is in front of us is a hard game to play, even for adults. Maybe the evidence suggests that our lover is cheating on us. Late hours at the office. Callers that hang up if we answer the phone. A lot less ardor in bed. We ought to think we are being cheated on. But to do so we would have to be able to hold on to the thought and not push it out of our mind. But that would require something we don't have—advanced pain-management techniques.

It takes discipline and hard work to make animals like us capable of thought or belief. We are fantasists, always flickering backward and forward between perceiving and imagining. Dreams do not occur only in bed at night. They are woven into the fabric of our waking lives. We wouldn't survive if they weren't. The pleasures they give us are vital to our energies: "Intervals of dreaming help us to stand up under days of work."[17] Intervals of reading, looking at paintings, listening to music, watching movies do the same. "The greatness and the indispensability of art," Nietzsche says, "lies precisely in its being able to produce the appearance of a simpler world, a shorter solution of the riddle of life. No one who suffers from life can do without this appearance, just as no one can do without sleep. . . . Art exists *so that the bow shall not break*."[18]

Like inner-Daddy, the prelinguistic sound <Daddy> or <Da Da> is a sort of surrogate or doppelgänger for Daddy himself. And just as the child learns to play fantasy and then reality with inner-Daddy, he learns to play language with that sound. But language is part of reality, not an isolated game of its own. It is by being included in reality that sounds like <Daddy>—the precursors of words—get their life. Language relates to the world because the world is where we language-users live.

Inner-Daddy escapes from the child's omnipotent control when it falls under the influence of the real Daddy and the child's increasing ability to experience him perceptually. It is the same with the sound <Daddy>. When the child plays reality with it, he has to use it as others do, since he is playing with them and trying to coordinate his behavior with theirs. If he tries to do things with it that aren't allowed in the game, the other children will correct him: "You can't be Daddy. You're too small. You're the baby. You be in the playpen."

In the mirror story, it was the mother's love that gave the child's image back to him as something he wanted to be. It provided the glue that stuck one to the other. Here it is the child's desire to play with other children—his need for their love and approval—that sticks <Daddy> to Daddy himself. If the seam holds, the sound <Daddy> becomes the word "Daddy," and the child now has a word in his vocabulary whose meaning—or part of whose meaning—he knows.

It's like using aliases for a computer file: when you click on a word, a file opens. But because the alias is much smaller, it can be used in ways the file itself cannot. Most of the time, in speaking, we use words not files. That is one reason we are able to talk so fast. But if we need to look into the file—for instance, if someone asks us what a word means—we can.

What we discover when we do look is a body of information—of common and not-so-common knowledge—which can be hierarchically organized. At level one, there is the sort of information you find in an ordinary (compact) dictionary. If you know how to play language, and you have that information, you count as knowing the meaning of the word. But meaning also has many other levels. At level two, there is what you find in an encyclopedia. And at some level above that, there is the file that contains new information provided by the relevant experts.

Take gravity. Experts are still disputing about its nature: Is it a special force? A warp in space-time? Some form of the strong or weak electromagnetic forces? Love is similar—but different. There are self-described experts on it—psychiatrists, sexologists, professors of gender or cultural or queer studies, authors of self-help books—but none who enjoy the cultural authority of an Einstein. Still, what they tell us about love gets included in the relevant files (think of Freud). When we use the word "love," when we think about love, how the word moves and where it wants to go are affected by their views.

Beyond the ordinary dictionaries, there are others: thesauruses, etymological dictionaries, dictionaries of quotations, concordances, public and private histories of the use of words. The swastika was a symbol like any other until the Nazis so contaminated it that it became as unusable as the word "nigger." So the historical associations of a word, whether in our collective history or in our personal histories, need a place in the filing system. Poets and writers use this information, but so do reflective speakers generally. Besides, we need it to explain free association—the unconscious use of words.

When we become sufficiently skilled at using "Daddy" that we use it even in thought and fantasy, inner-Daddy still gets pulled along by it, like a file attached to an alias. Much of what is in that file is written in a language we no longer speak fluently—the language of sucking in and pushing out, in which functional equivalents are treated as the very same thing. But it still exerts a subtle influence on the way we use the alias—the word. Maybe it affects how we see fathers or how we think the role of father has to be played. Maybe it even makes it hard for us to imagine ourselves playing that role or having children of our own.

When we learn to play language, it becomes a way—maybe *the* way—in which reality influences our mind and behavior. Language brings—or has the potential to bring—our developing minds under the sway of the accumulated wisdom and folly of our entire culture and its long history. And with all that comes the way we play the game of love—a game our parents have been playing with each other and with us from the beginning.

This love story—which is woven from the materials about love in the files our society attaches to the word "love"—we may call *conventional love*. When we love, we—improvising to some extent—act it out. In the files each of us ends up attaching to that word as a result of our earliest lessons in love, however, lies a different story: *infantile love*. Unlike its conventional descendant, infantile love is learned in a context of total helplessness and dependence on another. But life-and-death situations heighten and intensify experience and make it more memorable: in wars, and in games that simulate them, the heart beats faster. If, as we live out the complex story encoded in both files, both sorts of love are being played more or less simultaneously, reality somewhat satisfies our infantile desires, our experience is infused with the intense pleasures of infancy, and we feel vigorous and alive.

Infantile experiences are a store of energy, therefore, which can be exploited to vivify the humdrum later on. "So few of the hours of life," Samuel Johnson writes, "are filled up with objects adequate to the mind of man, and so frequently are we in want of present pleasure or employment, that we are forced to have recourse every moment to the past and future for supplemental satisfactions, and relieve the vacuity of our being, by recollection of former passages, or anticipation of events to come."[19] When we grow old, the need for such supplemental satisfactions itself grows, as the objects around us become ever less adequate to minds attuned to others that have vanished:

> Perhaps being old is having lighted rooms
> Inside your head, and people in them, acting.
> People you know, yet can't quite name; each looms
> Like a deep loss restored, from known doors turning,
> Setting down a lamp, smiling from a stair, extracting
> A known book from shelves; or sometimes only
> The rooms themselves, chairs and a fire burning,
> The blown bush at the window, or the sun's
> Faint friendliness on the wall some lonely
> Rain-ceased midsummer evening. That is where they live:
> Not here and now, but where all happened once.[20]

My own ninety-year-old mother often thinks that I am her (long dead) younger brother, unable to see in my bearded face that of her beloved son. Yet her face, once fretted with anxieties, has taken on its youthful beauty again. Where she is is better, happier, than where I see her being. Lucky her! The lighted rooms are not always so cozy.

When conventional love frustrates infantile love, what we fantasize about, dream about, wish for, gets split off from what we are really doing and the energy and pleasure that should be enlivening reality are invested elsewhere. (The frustrated wife becomes the ardent bridge-player.) Infantile love doesn't get explored or developed, and conventional love begins to seem cold and unsatisfactory and real life with it. Worse still, conventional love may invariably so frustrate infantile love that it becomes too painful to sustain. Infantile love can enliven; it can also deaden and destroy.

Infantile love can overheat conventional love, making it seem better than it is. It can cause love to get involved in other games, such as art or sports or science, and find more satisfaction there than in love for another person. "Man's creative struggle, his search for wisdom and truth, is a love story."[21] Infantile love can even affect deliberation and decision making. When situations are sufficiently complex, the best we can do is try on a role in fantasy to see how it fits. But just because it is in fantasy that we try it on, the influence of infantile love on it is considerable. Our reflective assessment of a relationship may be positive. Yet in our fantasies things keep going wrong. We reach impasses that frustrate and depress. We have dreams that tire us out and leave us with less energy for the real thing. We flicker off into depressing day-dreams and in reality our desire weakens.

A relationship may offer so much infantile satisfaction, indeed, that when we do try it on in fantasy, it seems ideal, while in reality it seems not to work at all. Yet fantasy may win out and we may go on with it anyway: "We fall in love for a smile, a look, a shoulder. That is enough; then in the long hours of hope or sorrow, we fabricate a person, we compose a character. And when later on we see much of the beloved being, we can no more, whatever the cruel reality that confronts us, divest the woman with that look, that shoulder, of the sweet nature and loving character with which we endowed her than we can, when she has grown old, eliminate her youthful face from a person whom we have known from girlhood."[22]

A mother's love for her child attaches his mirror image to him—but with a twist. It attaches it to him as someone he wants to be, not as someone he is. For the cohesive-ness, integrity, and clarity he sees in the image actually conflict with his sense of dependence and lack of coordi-nation. Then, as he learns language, he learns to use the word "I" not only in place of that inner self-image but also in place of baby—an actor in the public drama of life. So the word acquires a kind of shifting reference for him. It is who he really is, who he wants to be, and who they—the other players of language—say he is and want him to be. "You" forces an acknowledging "I." The linguistic unity of the word "I"—its grammatical identity—is like the tantalizing but illusory integrity and clarity of the mirror image.

Just as there are files attached to the word "love," there are similar files attached to the word "I"—a word we "set up," Nietzsche claims, "at the point at which our ignorance begins, at which we can see no further."[23] Somewhere among these files are the theories of experts on the "I"—psychologists, psychiatrists, philosophers, priests. So the question of who I am falls under the sway of whichever of them happens to have authority where and when I speak. When priests were oracles, I was my immortal soul, my spiritual self. Now I am something else. Who I am is as much—and as little—under the authority of others as what love is, and what I must do if I am to love. In our wanting to be loved, it not only isn't obvious what we want to have happen—it isn't obvious to whom we want to have it happen.

4

ANXIETY AND THE ETHICS OF INTIMACY

Anxiety is a psychological reaction to the unbearable. We experience it when we want to push something out or pull something in to fill the emptiness—but can't. So containment is crucial. And because it is, anxiety is primitive. It belongs, first and foremost, to a mind that thinks in an alimentary way. But the "primitive mind is, in the fullest meaning of the word, imperishable."[1] It stays around, like the reptilian brain, dealing even with adult situations in its own characteristic fashion.

The unbearable, too, is rooted in the primitive and the infantile; somatic pain is its most familiar exemplar. But while such pain may be—or involve—a sensation, pain in general (for example, the pain of loss) isn't necessarily a sensation. Instead, it is a prominent member of the class of things from which we natively recoil. The nauseating is another, as is the itchy. What we natively recoil from, we try to rid ourselves of. If it is inside us, like colic or a painful lump of stool, we try to push it out. We can learn to bear such things, but natively we just recoil. If they get attached to something else, we try to push it out, too, and find it difficult to attend to or keep in mind. Pleasure, likewise, is a prominent member of the class of things (including some sensations) to which we natively cling. The joyful, the amusing, the interesting are others. As we natively shun somatic pain, we natively cling to somatic pleasure and want to keep it—and anything it gets attached to—inside.

In the phenomenon of such attachment, familiar to all parents and puppy owners and exploited by them, lie the beginnings of an account of how pleasure (or pain) can be shifted from a site where it can be experienced (penis) to one where it can't (finger), and so of an explanation of the initially paradoxical idea of pleasures (or pains) that are hollow or imaginary: we posit the pleasure to explain the attachment.

Since we readily engage with what we want to keep inside, pleasure is natively an antidote to anxiety. That is one reason we can comfort suffering children and puppies by stroking and holding them. The mere fact that we natively cling to pleasure doesn't make it an intrinsic good, however. If it persists too long, or becomes too intense, it threatens us with loss of control—with dissolution, with breaking into pieces—and so produces anxiety of its own. But because it can counteract anxiety, pleasure is at least an important extrinsic good.

In these simple facts lie the roots of a complex structure and a complex phenomenology. Pains and pleasures may enter our lives in the guise of somatic sensations. But these are just the embryos of beings whose mature forms no more resemble them than butterflies do caterpillars. A good story about pleasure and pain, as a result, has to be a *Bildungsroman*.

Initially a matter of what can be inside my skin envelope, containment soon becomes a matter of what can be inside my self. But the self is indefinitely enrichable—as it is impoverishable—by culture and experience: contempt doesn't directly attack my body, but it does attack me. How I can be harmed is in part a matter of who I am. Who I am is in part socially determined. So what can be in my body—or what can go into it—can come to be partly determined by who I am. When a friend's half-sister was a child, her mother found her eating her feces. Later, when she was being toilet trained, there was a period when she wouldn't wipe herself because she was disgusted at the idea of getting poop on her hands. Initially, we gag only when our body won't hold something in. Then we gag when the thought of having something in or on it disgusts us.

Like containment, impotence is initially a matter of the body, then a matter of the self, then a matter of the body as imagined: I can't pick that up because I'm not strong enough or coordinated enough; I can't pick it up because I can't overcome my disgust at touching it. Anxiety, tied to impotence and containment, extends its territory as they extend theirs, and so has a prominent place among the "self-born mockers of man's enterprise" Yeats talks about.[2] But it is also part of the energy that drives the enterprise itself.

We enrich ourselves by taking in new material. We also do it by learning—often at the hands of love—how to keep in old unbearable material we were formerly able only to push out. The unbearable marks the boundary of the self, the area from which we exclude strangers—the area of intimacy, the area we invite our lover to explore. It is also the area from which we exclude ourselves, the area outside our boundaries, the area to which we invite our lover to take us—even if going there is difficult. That is why love involves "a notable and non-trivial suspension of some, if not all, rules of disgust."[3] If a stranger invites me to kiss her ass, she is expressing contempt by inviting me to go somewhere and do something generally found disgusting. If my lover invites me to do the same thing, she may well be placing what is generally found disgusting in the realm of the erotic, in the realm of the beautiful. So the anus, as what William Ian Miller calls "the gateway to the most private, the most personal space of all," is a perennial temptation to love.[4]

Kant talks in one of his lectures about a mistrust of others that leads us not only to "cover up our weaknesses, so as not to be ill thought of," but also to "withhold our opinions." It is only if we can get rid of this mistrust, he says, "and impart our feelings to the other," that we can achieve complete friendship, complete love. To accomplish this, however, a powerful anxiety must be overcome, namely, that our friend or lover might feel disgust rather than love for what full disclosure on our part would reveal to her. But in a rational person the anxiety will always defeat the love: "Even to our best friend, we must not discover ourselves as we naturally are and know ourselves to be, for that would be a nasty business." Then comes reason's counsel of despair: "We must so conduct ourselves towards a friend that it does no harm if he were to become our enemy; we must give him nothing to use against us." Love—including self-love—is impossible, given how we naturally are.[5]

What about our natural selves, we might wonder, is so nasty that even a best friend could not be expected to tolerate it? A revealing simile shows Kant's thoughts to be Millerian: "Domestic nastiness is confined to the privy, and we refrain from inviting a friend into the bedroom, where the chamber-pots are, though he knows we have them, just as he does himself, lest we get into the habit of doing so and corrupt our taste. In just the same way, we conceal our faults." Though we certainly have many other "characteristics and tendencies that are objectionable to others," those exposed in the bathroom and bedroom are evidently paradigm cases.[6]

The truth in these anxious reflections on love is that sharing hearts' secrets is a two-sided game—if for no other reason than that the anxieties of one-sided sharing are usually too great. When each confides, however, each has equal reason not to divulge to a third party. Sharing is both an act of love and a way of arming love against its enemies. If my lover could use what she knows to hurt me, I have a reason to do what will keep her loving me—and vice versa. If each of us is disgusting, disclosure is more likely to comfort than to threaten. When enough people go public with their "disgusting" qualities, in fact, these often get transformed into a badge of solidarity.

By encouraging us to disclose more and more of what we would otherwise hide, intimate love—almost paradoxically—gives rise to many of the anxieties for which it promises to be the cure. In this way, as no doubt in others, it creates the conditions of its own reproduction. When the anxieties aroused by the threat of its demise exceed those aroused by its continuity, love goes on—everything else being equal.

When love is responsive to or based on genuinely good qualities (or socially valued ones), this may seem bound to be the case. But the supposed inevitability conceals an anxiety—and an imagined palliative: if I don't come up to snuff, I won't be loved (anxiety); if I do, I will be (palliative). What both fail to register is that qualities will be found good by a lover whose peculiar anxieties they help transmute or assuage. Often, and for obvious reasons, there is substantial overlap between these qualities and genuinely good ones: we are typically made very anxious by selfishness, cruelty, injustice, and inconstancy. But the goodness of these qualities—if they possess it—is not what makes them peculiarly relevant to love.

Consider Ray and Iris Finch, the central characters in Norman Rush's novel *Mortals*. Without telling Ray, Iris has begun seeing, in a semi-psychoanalytic capacity, an iconoclastic black physician named Davis Morel. When

Ray senses that something is going on, Iris determines to be forthright: "She was talking about it because it was important for her to tell the truth about things, for her sake and for his." But as she tells her story, Ray becomes anxious: "Something was coming that he didn't want to hear. . . . It was excruciating." He is sure that Iris has fallen in love with Morel and is about to tell him so. Soon he can bear the suspense no longer: "He had to know what was coming. It was, and it didn't matter why it was coming, it didn't matter why it was coming, whether it was the issue of their childlessness aggravated again via her sister cleverly devising to get pregnant by an absolute fool, or if it was the first cold wind of menopause beginning to blow, or if it was boredom with him versus the black glamour of the black bastard he had the power to destroy utterly."

When Iris becomes aware of Ray's state, she strives to set his mind at rest. "'You poor thing,' she said, 'I am *in pain* if you thought I was thinking of anything like that. *Please.* Oh my poor *thing*.'" But despite her assurances, his anxiety remains unassuaged: "He thought, She wants Morel, despite all this she does, she won't do it with him, but this is where we are . . . she prefers him . . . I'm more interesting . . . not that she can see it, but I am." It becomes so acute, indeed, that when Iris says, "We love each other," he still thinks she is referring to herself and Morel: "He flinched. He felt weak. It was too much." "'I mean us, *us*,' she said, clearly alarmed. She touched his face."

In the end, Ray's anxious intimations turn out to be on to something. Iris *is* smitten with Morel, though con-

fident (unjustifiably, as it turns out) that she can keep
things under control: "I'm going to see him *and* nothing
is going to happen. I love you and you're my husband.
But I'm going to go to him and when he's helped me I'm
going to stop. Helped me, to my satisfaction." "I feel vacant," Ray responds. "This is making me feel vacant."
"I'm very sorry if it is," Iris replies. "It shouldn't." Hearing
the new toughness that is part of her resolve to tell the
truth—a resolve which is itself a result of her therapy with
Morel—Ray's anxiety increases yet again: "I am nowhere,
he thought." Iris briskly restates her reassurance: "'Nothing is going to happen. I am swearing this to you. I swear
it.' She pressed her palm to her sternum, like a diva, but
in all seriousness." The theatricality of the gesture and
Iris' admission of interest have an effect on Ray—an effect
that is temporarily devastating: "Nonsense was pushing
its way into his mind. They began to begin to be gone, he
thought, three times, making himself stop when he felt
the phrase entrenching itself."[7]

In response to Iris' honesty, Ray self-aggrandizes ("I'm
more interesting"), affects omnipotence ("I have the
power to destroy him utterly"), senses conspiracies ("her
sister cleverly devising"), blames hormonal changes ("the
first cold wind of menopause"), doubts Iris' love for him
. . . until finally his anxiety creates an inner vacancy for
nonsense to fill. Instead of causing love to develop, honesty here renders it infantile and unbearable.

Like a born-again Christian's faith in Jesus, Iris' newly
minted commitment to honesty is no doubt a bit strident. To tell these truths to *Ray* with any hope of achiev-

ing uptake, she would first need to prepare the ground carefully. Had she done so (and had Ray not been quite so much of a control freak and a fussbudget), he might have already seen in her relationship with Morel—as to some extent he does by the novel's conclusion—not the end of love, but something more like its new, more grown-up beginning. The value of honesty in the abstract is not, we are made aware, the measure of its intimate value. What measures that are is its effects on the lover's anxieties.

Margaret Schlegel in *Howards End* understands this perfectly, and so is a careful ground-preparer. When Henry Wilcox proposes to her, it is, as she thinks, "a strange love scene," in part because he never says he loves her. "He might have done it if she had pressed him—as a matter of duty, perhaps; England expects every man to open his heart once; but the effort would have jarred him, and never, if she could avoid it, should he lose those defences that he had chosen to raise against the world."[8]

Later, Margaret learns that during his first marriage, to her friend Ruth Wilcox, Henry had a mistress. Though this was not her tragedy, but Ruth's, it still shocks Margaret deeply: "She was too bruised to speak to Henry; she could pity him, and even determine to marry him, but as yet all lay too deep in her heart for speech. On the surface the sense of his degradation was too strong. She could not command voice or look, and the gentle words that she forced out through her pen seemed to proceed from some other person." The words are these: "'My dearest boy,' she began, 'this is not to part us. It is everything or nothing, and I mean it to be nothing. It happened long before we ever met, and even if it had happened since, I should be writing the same, I hope. I do understand.'"

What Margaret has written is already tactful and loving, but her knowledge of Henry leads her to see in it phrases that must be excised: "She crossed out 'I do understand'; it struck a false note. Henry could not bear to be understood. She also crossed out 'It is everything or nothing.' Henry would resent so strong a grasp of the situation." If Henry is to accept his fiancée's knowledge about his past and get beyond it, his defenses must be circumvented, not activated. Though the careful note is never in fact sent, writing it fore-arms Margaret somewhat for the subsequent conversation.[9]

This begins with Henry precipitately releasing Margaret from her engagement. "I'm a bad lot," he says, "and must be left at that." "Expelled from his old fortress," Forster comments, "Mr Wilcox was building a new one. He could no longer appear respectable . . . , so he defended himself instead in a lurid past. It was not true repentance." That this past makes no difference to Margaret is itself disconcerting to Henry, since it suggests a level of sexual understanding incompatible with his conception of womanly propriety: "He was annoyed with Miss Schlegel here. He would have preferred her to be prostrated by the blow, or even to rage. Against the tide of his sin flowed the feeling that she was not altogether womanly. Her eyes gazed too straight; they had read books that are suitable for men only." It is to the contrast between her (suspect) purity and his "strong but furtive passions" that Henry is reluctantly but irresistibly led.

The fortress of the lurid past requires the assured purity of the assailant.

"You, with your sheltered life, and refined pursuits, and friends and books, you and your sister, and women like you—I say, how can you guess the temptations that lie round a man?" "It is difficult for us," Margaret replies; "but if we are worth marrying we do guess." She is forgetting, we sense, how little Henry can bear to be understood. He needs his past to be lurid. He needs to feel himself "a bad lot." To be forgiven by someone he sees—and needs to see—as pure is bound to be troubling.

As Henry tells the story of his affair "bit by bit," however, Margaret remembers how much he needs his defenses intact if he is to function: "Now and then he asked her whether she could possibly forgive him, and she answered: 'I have already forgiven you, Henry.' She chose her words carefully, and so saved him from panic. She played the girl, until he could rebuild his fortress and hide his soul from the world." Panic. It is just what Iris, by her too strident honesty, fails to prevent in Ray.

In the event, Margaret is successful—"when the butler came to clear away Henry was in a very different mood."[10] But even her art of love has its limitations. Her sister Helen has a brief affair with Leonard Bast, the husband of Henry's ex-mistress, Jacky Bast. (Not the happiest contrivance in a somewhat overly contrived plot.) Pregnant with Bast's child, she wishes to spend the night in Howards End, the house that Henry has acquired through the death of his first wife. (It is not without significance that to acquire it he had to conceal her dying bequest of it to

Margaret herself.) The scene in which Margaret asks him to grant her sister's request shows her first as adapting her old stratagem of deference to his defenses. But these now prove to be the very obstacle she must overcome to help her sister. "I cannot treat her as if nothing has happened," Henry responds to her, "I should be false to my position in society if I did." "Margaret," Forster tells us, "controlled herself for the last time." Helen's request, she allows, is unreasonable. However, it is the request of an unhappy girl, who tomorrow will go to Germany and trouble society no longer. Then comes Margaret's own more pointed renewal of the request: "Tonight she asks to sleep in your empty house—a house which you do not care about, and which you have not occupied for over a year. May she? Will you give my sister leave? Will you forgive her—as you hope to be forgiven, and as you have actually been forgiven? Forgive her for one night only. That will be enough."

Some hint of Margaret's meaning may have dawned on Henry. "If so, Forster says, "he blotted it out. Straight from his fortress he answered: 'I seem rather unaccommodating, but I have some experience of life, and know how one thing leads to another. I am afraid that your sister had better sleep at the hotel. I have my children and the memory of my dear wife to consider. I am sorry, but see that she leaves my house at once." The irony of "my house" is terrible, though Margaret is as yet ignorant of it. But the mention of Ruth is too much. "In reply," she says, "may I mention Mrs Bast?"

Though the fortress's doors are rattled, Henry's face remains impassive. It is Margaret who is "transfigured." She rushes to him and seizes his hands:

> "Not any more of this!" she cried. "You shall see the connection if it kills you, Henry! You have had a mistress—I forgave you. My sister has a lover—you drive her from the house. Do you see the connection? Stupid, hypocritical, cruel— oh, contemptible!—a man who insults his wife when she's alive and cants with her memory when she's dead. A man who ruins a woman for his pleasure, and casts her off to ruin other men. . . . These men are you. You can't recognize them, because you cannot connect. I've had enough of your unweeded kindness. I've spoilt you long enough. All your life you have been spoilt. . . . No one has ever told you what you are—muddled, criminally muddled. Men like you use repentance as a blind, so don't repent. Only say to yourself: 'What Helen has done, I've done.'"

It is for naught. Margaret has run up against defenses whose strength exceeds that of her own over-stressed self control. Henry hears the mention of Mrs. Bast not as an invitation to connect, but as blackmail—"scarcely a pretty weapon for a wife to use against her husband." And against blackmail his defenses are proof. "My rule through life," he says, "has been never to pay the least attention to threats." When Margaret lets go his hands—she has been clutching them throughout—he leaves her, "wiping first one and then the other on his handkerchief." It is Henry at his nadir of appeal.[11]

In the novel's last act, Henry's son Charles is threatened with prison for the manslaughter of Leonard Bast. "I don't know what to do—what to do," Henry tells Margaret, who is the process of leaving him for Helen and Germany. "I'm broken—I'm ended." "No sudden warmth arose in her," Forster tells us. "She did not see that to break him was her only hope. She did not enfold the sufferer in her arms. But all through that day and the next a new life began to move." It is a rare authorial misstep. For Margaret, as we have seen, *cannot* break Henry. Only from within the fortress of his position in society—threatened now by the prosecution of his son—can the walls of his defenses be breached. When Charles is actually sentenced to prison, *then* "Henry's fortress actually gave way." His earlier claim to be "ended" (echoed by Helen a few pages later: "I'm ended," she says) is an exaggeration. Margaret's love can give both of them new life.[12]

As Forster speculates about Margaret on the eve of her marriage, he raises the following question: "To have no illusions and yet to love—what stronger surety can a woman find?"[13] By the end of the novel, he has answered it. The beloved must be reachable by that love. He must not be, as Henry is, so immured in the defensive fortress his anxieties have constructed that love cannot find him. Margaret recognizes this, too. Her love, in whose transformative power she once exulted—"Henry must have it as he liked, for she loved him, and someday she would use her love to make him a better man"—she now sees as much more limited in its powers. "No doubt I have done a little towards straightening the tangle," she says to Helen, "but things that I can't phrase have helped me."[14]

Among these things, Forster thinks, is Howards End itself and the English countryside that is threatened by the expansion of London. The "craze for motion," for excitement, is taking over, but there is still hope that it "may be followed by a civilization that won't be a movement, because it will rest on the earth."[15] Though clouded by nostalgic pastoral, Forster's point is important. Different sorts of love need different sorts of environments—different sorts of Lebensraum—if they are to thrive.

When we say that love is whatever develops from, and somewhat recapitulates, a child's relationship with his mother, we are being descriptive. For what develops in that way can apparently be something objectively very bad, either for the adult the child becomes or for the person he loves. When we say that love is "the ultimate form of recognition one grants to superlative values,"[16] or that it involves "taking pleasure in (the thought of) the existence and well-being of the loved individual,"[17] we are saying that when our early relationship with our mother develops properly—another normative notion—that is what it develops into. There is good love and bad love, in other words—love and other things that are corrupted or perverted forms of it.

Once we introduce anxiety into the equation, however, this picture is destabilized. Maybe it is true that we *ought* to love the best people best, but, like Hetta Carbury in Trollope's *The Way We Live Now,* we typically don't.[18] The best people, after all, can make us—since we are less than best ourselves—unbearably anxious: "Surely, she will leave me when she sees me as I am." Maybe it is true, too, that we ought to feel pleasure at the thought of our lover's very existence. But, like Samuel Beckett, we may not. In one of his early lyrics he says:

> I would like my love to die
> and the rain to be falling on the graveyard
> and on me walking the streets
> mourning the first and last to love me.[19]

While our lover lives, our love can die. Another can take her place in our life or our place in hers. Were she in fact to die, maybe it would be a different story. But for now all there is is love—and an anxiety about its loss that makes pleasure in the existence of its object impossible.

Virtues are sometimes and plausibly conceived as safeguards against common human failings and temptations. We need courage because we are prone to fear, and to the weakness of will it can cause; temperance or moderation because we are prone to lust and gluttony; truthfulness because we are prone to lie when the going gets tough.[20] So conceived, the virtues have the look of separate traits. But it is probably better to think of them as elements, only apparently distinct, in what David Shapiro calls a "style"—individual peaks, visible above the clouds, of a single mountain.[21] Someone with all the virtues has the virtuous—or morally good—style. He perceives, feels, thinks, and acts in a recognizable way—perhaps the way Aristotle's *phronimos,* or man of practical wisdom, does. His outer life has a distinctive look, his inner life a distinctive texture, his world a distinctive coloration. The courageous person, while he might have many other virtues, has a different style, one in which courage has pride of place.

An ethics of the more intimate self would focus not on these broad failings alone, but on the finer-grained and highly idiosyncratic anxieties of intimate life, and on the different character styles developed as defenses against them: obsessive-compulsive, hysterical, narcissistic, and so on. For each such style, we might imagine a corresponding account of what virtue might look like in someone with such a style. What, for example, would it look like in a narcissist? What trait or traits would prevent his characteristic defenses from making intimacy impossible?

Or, turning it around, what in his lover would enable her to breach those defenses without galvanizing his anxieties? What in her would be the counterparts of the tact, discretion, and clearsightedness in Zoë Cunningham? For it is in the nature of the virtues of intimacy, I think, that they be indexed to a particular relationship—a particular lover. What allows us safely to traverse the minefield of one lover's anxieties may not be successful with another's. Comfortable with Joe or Jack, she may be forever on edge with us.

Conscious, as we cannot help being, that "a man lives not only his personal life, as an individual, but also, consciously or unconsciously, the life of his epoch and his contemporaries," we would also need to index all these styles to different cultures and historical periods.[22] At that point, we would be able to see in some detail the different tensions and conflicts that exist in different times and places between being a good or virtuous person (a good actor on the public stage) and being a good or virtuous lover (a good actor on the intimate stage).

One such conflict, however, seems likely to appear in every case. It is well described by the psychoanalyst Donald Meltzer:

> The huge majority of caring parents, seeing all about them the misery of maladaptation, cannot help being primarily concerned, in their methods of upbringing, with armouring their children against the inhumanities inflicted on both the poorly adapted and on those whose naked sensitivity makes them vulnerable to the grossness of inconsiderate behaviour in casual and contractual relations. Similarly, our schools cannot resist the pressure from parents and government alike to direct their efforts toward producing employable grown-ups. One must see the facts without wishing to pretend that any alternative is close at hand. We wish to prepare our children for the beauties of intimacy but our anxieties for their survival overcome our judgement so that we find ourselves joining in the training process, knowing quite well

that it will dampen their thirst for knowledge
and constrict their openness to the beauties to
which they stand heir.[23]

Well-armored for combat in the larger public world, we
may find the virtues of intimacy difficult to cultivate—
difficult even to access.

5

JEALOUSY, PERVERSITY, AND OTHER LIABILITIES OF LOVE

According to Jean-Paul Sartre, "The lover does not desire to possess the beloved as one possesses a thing; he demands a special sort of appropriation. He wants to possess a freedom as freedom . . . but demands that this freedom as freedom should no longer be free. He wishes that the Other's freedom should determine itself to become love—and this not only at the beginning of the affair but at each instant—and at the same time he wants this same freedom to be captured *by itself,* to turn back upon itself, as in madness, as in a dream, so as to will its own captivity."[1] Though characteristically extreme, Sartre is surely on to something. What lover hasn't found himself with some such impossible wish? Yet, on reflection, the characterization seems to fit better one of love's common liabilities—jealous possessiveness—than love itself.

No surprise, therefore, to find that Sartre cites Proust's

Marcel (he means the narrator of *Remembrance of Things Past*) as if in corroboration of his account. For Marcel is often presented as a paradigm case of possessive jealousy. Indeed, he seems to present himself as such: "Jealousy is a demon that cannot be exorcised, but constantly appears in new incarnations. Even if we could succeed in exterminating them all, in keeping the beloved for ever, the Spirit of Evil would then adopt another form, more pathetic still, despair at having obtained fidelity only by force, despair at not being loved." Yet in Marcel's view the very unexorcisability of his jealousy—its inability, in the face of the beloved's freedom, to achieve its goal—is a good thing from the erotic point of view: "For just as in the beginning it is formed by desire, so afterwards love is kept in existence only by painful anxiety: I felt that part of Albertine's life eluded me. Love, in the pain of anxiety as in the bliss of desire, is a demand for a whole. It is born, and it survives, only if some part remains for it to conquer. We love only what we do not wholly possess." Jealousy keeps Marcel's love alive, therefore, even if in the process that love becomes "reciprocal torture."[2]

Reciprocal torture may sound simply pathological, but that should not blind us to Marcel's insight. Erotic desire is inextricably bound up with excitement; excitement with tantalization. Yet tantalization *is* a kind of torture—an "enlivening torture," as Adam Phillips calls it, that rekindles and refreshes desire, and so sustains it.[3] Since flirtation, as a kind of tantalization, requires an answering jealousy, jealousy, too, can function to keep desire alive.

In one of her poems, Eavan Boland speaks of "the code marriage makes of passion—*duty, dailiness, routine.*"[4] Flirtation and jealousy disrupt this code. They reveal the threat to repetition that is always there, even if disguised by routine. More interestingly, they reveal the correlative threat *of* repetition—of boredom, complacency, indifference, insensitivity, blindness. They help to open up a space in which the aims and goals of a relationship, instead of being given by the very idea of marriage, intimacy, or sexuality, are to be worked out, made up, improvised.

Though jealousy can enliven desire, its association with possessiveness may seem to constitute a liability too great to be outweighed even by so large a potential benefit. To the extent that flirtation needs jealousy, it too may seem to suffer guilt by association—jealousy seeking to keep what flirtation threatens with loss. What this critique overlooks is that while jealousy can be "greediness stimulated by fear," it can also be "emulation sharpened by fear."[5] The greedy lover seeks to keep all of his lover for himself; the emulous one to keep his relationship with her in excellent condition. The former is led by a rival to tighten his grip; the latter to love better. A flirt who seeks to incite greed implicitly seeks to be more thoroughly possessed, and so is party to his lover's possessiveness. One who incites emulation, on the other hand, seeks what emulation seeks—a better, more alive relationship. The loss that emulous jealousy fears, therefore, isn't the loss of a person who, as free, cannot be possessed, but the loss—through neglect—of the loving relationship itself.

A lover's presence in our life is pervasive. Without her,

the plot of ourselves, the sense we make, threatens to un-ravel: "The beloved for the lover empties the world of hope (the world that doesn't include her)."[6] When a rival for her affections appears, therefore, proleptic mourning occurs in us for her (she will be dead to us . . .) and also for ourselves (. . . and so we will be as if dead). At the same time, we imagine her presence in the rival's life—"Someone else feeling her breasts and cunt, / Someone else drowned in that lash-wide stare."[7] We feel anger toward the rival for the harm he threatens; envy at the success that may be his. We feel anger at ourselves for our own contribution to our potential loss; anger at our lover for her contribution. It is a potent cocktail of feelings. The risk involved in galvanizing it, even in order to enliven desire, is consequently great. The risk of finding that love has died for want of enlivening is equally life-threatening, of course, though the continued presence of the lover tends to make it seem less so.

When we think about the risks and rewards of jealousy, we are forced to think about its role in different psychological styles. In Marcel, for example, it proves so destructive of his relationship with Albertine, that love—as something felt for another person—is abandoned as too painful. "My love was not so much a love for her," he tells us when she is gone, "as a love in myself," with "no real connexion" to anyone else.[8] What once promised to link Marcel to something outside himself now links him solely to the contents of his own mind—contents for which other people have become "merely showcases." In a different style, that would be no more than a record of descent into narcissistic solipsism. In Marcel—in Proust—it has a very different outcome. Precisely because nothing can relieve his jealousy of Albertine, it can keep revealing "layer after layer" of the stuff of which he is made—a revelation that becomes *Remembrance of Things Past* itself.[9] "Proust could afford to find human relationships insufficient—or at any rate he could make Marcel do so—because he knew he was to find an answer in his writing."[10]

The jealousy Maggie Verver feels toward Charlotte Stant, in Henry James's *Golden Bowl,* is a component of a very different psychological style and has very different consequences. By making Maggie doubt "the wonderful little world" of her wealth and privilege, it makes her realize that though Amerigo is her husband, "all the while she really *hasn't* had him." The realization is disagreeable, naturally. But, as Fanny Assingham sees, it "*had* to be disagreeable" in order to show Maggie "a little where she is . . . to make her sit up . . . to make her decide to live."[11] The decision to live, to "risk the cracks," whether in golden bowls, in princely husbands, or in life itself, transforms Maggie's jealousy into a "painful rite of passage to the difficult reconstitution of herself in loving."[12] Whereas Marcel's jealousy causes him to see only Albertine's real or imagined betrayal, Maggie's causes her to see her own defects as partly responsible for Amerigo's threatened loss. Loving, she comes to realize, isn't a matter of possession, of storing away in a vault, but of a dynamic engagement fraught with pain and risk.

In Maggie, jealousy acts as a force of erotic development: she loves Amerigo better by being able to work through it. In Marcel, it destroys love—at any rate as an interpersonal relationship. Depending on the resources available to the person in whom it occurs, jealousy can be an erotic disaster or an erotic boon. This may not be only a matter of individual psychology, however. It may also depend on history. The Victorians, according to Steven Kern, "viewed jealousy as a disease to be avoided." In response to it, "they typically chose denial, flight, self-pity, or, in extreme instances, the retribution of murder or the 'satisfaction' of dueling." In each case, the response "projected the source of the grievance onto either the 'unfaithful' beloved or the 'third party' and therefore avoided reflecting on any sources of the grievance" within the jealous person himself. There is a sense, then, in which the Victorian understanding of jealousy puts a Marcel-like or Maggie-like response beyond the pale. For jealousy to be seen as "not so much an affliction or an evil" but more as "an unavoidable and important challenge, essential to retrieving oneself as a self and to tempering love as nonpossessive and free," profound social changes—as well as profound psychological ones—had to take place.[13]

When Freud discovered that "the sexual instinct and the sexual object are merely soldered together," and "come apart in the perversions," the very idea of sexuality as an instinct was undercut—and with it the distinction between normal and perverse sexuality, as this had previously been understood.[14] If the natural object of the penis isn't ejaculation in a vagina, a penis whose object is ejaculation in a mouth or anus is just a penis that gets its pleasure somewhere else. It isn't a normal or perverse penis, just a penis with different tastes. Ditto for a clitoris that gets its pleasure from a tongue rather than—more awkwardly, given its position—from a penis. Pleasure is pleasure, not an identity card.

What Freud did without fully realizing it—"genius is always ahead even of itself"—was to pave the way for the *demoralizing* of sexuality, while at the same time giving it a much larger say in who we are.[15] Bulimia and dipsomania, once thought of as perversions of the nutritive instinct, according to Freud result from the so-called libidinization of the alimentary function. (Think of the erotic vomiting described earlier.) Even how we eat and drink and go to the bathroom can reveal our sexuality. "Few neurotics," Freud writes, "are to be found without their special scatological practices, ceremonies, and so on, which they keep carefully secret."[16] Few non-neurotics for that matter.

But what I do with my mouth or anus or penis doesn't tell you whether I'm good or bad, or whether what I'm making is love or something else. The answer to the question Beckett's Molloy asks—"Is it true love, in the rectum?"—is that its being in the rectum doesn't tell you.[17] We are closer, thanks to Freud, to a time "when we can think to ourselves, 'How do I love thee; let me count the ways,' and no longer fear our possible perversion."[18] But only closer.

The polymorphous sexuality of the child is called "perversity" by Freud, because of the influence the sexual instinct still exerts on his thought, notwithstanding his own fatal deconstruction of it. The same unfortunate influence is what leads him to elevate "heterosexual genitality to a unique position, as if it were the only aspect of infantile sexuality fit to survive into adult life."[19] Like vaginal orgasms and death by masturbation, it is an idea that ought to seem silly or quaint to us as post-Freudians, but for all sorts of reasons continues not to.

If sexual perversity does exist, then, it can't be anything like what continues to get so (mis-)called. It can't simply be a matter of what sexual acts we perform, what we perform them with, or with whom we perform them. But what, then, *is* it a matter of?

A child typically feels an embryonic form of loving gratitude when his mother feeds, holds, or comforts him. When she doesn't—and there are bound to be occasions when she doesn't, human life being what it is—he typically feels an embryonic form of hate-filled envy instead.[20] His hunger is attacking him. He can't defend himself against it. His mother could defend him—so in that regard she is good—but she doesn't. And that reveals her as separate from him, not under his control. So he hates her as a good thing separate from himself. And that hatred is envy: "Envy is pained at seeing another have what it wants for itself."[21]

If, where love develops in us, envy exerts an overwhelming influence, we may be led to want not to destroy the things we love, but to sustain them in existence in order to compete enviously with them, and by doing so to reassure ourselves repeatedly that we do not need them or the good things (generosity, creativity, fullness of life, beauty) they have. In that case, our state of mind is in a genuine and intelligible sense perverse in its purpose, since it rejects whatever is good and alive, and aims instead "to create a world which is the negative of . . . the realm of good objects," a world of "the life-less, for whom the great anxieties of the living, time-bound, cannot exist."[22] A married couple having missionary-position vaginal intercourse may be sexual perverts, whereas a sadomasochistic lesbian couple anally fisting each other may not be. Queerness is no guarantee of perversion; "heteronormativity" no safeguard against it.

The painful oscillation between infantile love and hate or envy may also, as we have seen, cause a split between the good or gratifying mother and the bad or persecuting one. But a child really has only one—imperfect—mother, not a perfectly good one and a perfectly bad one. So as reality comes to exert more and more control over his mind—if that is what happens—he is faced with an integrative task. He must combine the good and bad mother into one.[23]

Suppose your baby is hungry and you are slow to respond. He begins to get terrified, overcome with anxiety. He can't cope. If you can, if his anxiety doesn't make you anxious too, you can diminish it. You can give him back his anxiety in more tolerable form. In time, he will learn to experience and work through it instead of being undone by it. Frustration, and the envy and hatred it arouses, will then become less of a threat to loving gratitude, which will itself come to be experienced as involving—without being too threatened by—envy and hate. If you *can't* cope, however, envy and hate will tend to poison love and make it unbearable, unfeelable. This is one significant way in which "man hands on misery to man."[24]

Embryonic love and hate—pure love and pure hate—are feelings that haven't yet come to grips with imperfect reality. Mature love, by contrast, is impure—bound up with envy and hate. When we love that way, we don't experience those destructive feelings—at least not for very long—as the death of love. We can tolerate them, and so don't have to push out the love in order to rid ourselves of them.

We are inclined to talk about love as if it were a purely good thing. This is hardly surprising, since our ordinary concept of love represents it as such. Yet our ordinary concepts are sometimes distorting of reality. Freud discovered long ago that someone suffering from hysterical paralysis of the arm—the part of the body marked off by the ordinary concept of an arm—isn't suffering from a disease of the anatomical arm, since no paralysis could affect only the former, given the latter's actual musculature and neural structure.[25] He also showed, more controversially, that our ordinary concept of the sexual doesn't mark off a psychological unity. If we generalize his discoveries, they ought to make us skeptical—anyway, noncomplacent—about our ordinary concepts. Conventional love is indeed the opposite of envy and hate, and precludes them. The psychological reality the concept of it points to, however, may be more complex and more accommodating—a "crooked thing," as Yeats calls it.[26]

This is something to keep in mind when, in the face

of love's confusions, we are tempted to divide and conquer. Sexual love, parental love, fraternal love, friendship, agape, love of country, love of sports . . . Introduce enough distinctions, we think, and the confusions will all be resolved. But that supposes that these distinctions are not themselves manifestations of confusions and anxieties—that they are not, in part, defenses. When we try to live them out, we are likely to be made vividly aware of just how contentious that supposition is.

A good mother who can deal with her child's anxiety gives him back his self-image as something good, something to love and identify with. A bad mother gives it back to him as something bad, something to hate and disown. But if her love is schizoid, if it tends to become hate when her baby doesn't respond appropriately to her loving, his self-image is given back to him as something that easily switches from good to bad. That is why such love "depletes the ego."[27] For when someone experiences his desires, wishes, or qualities as loved in such a flickering way, he is unable to identify with them in a stable manner. Consequently, what he brings to bear on himself and others as love will itself be bound to flicker.

No mother is perfect. So no one can have a love for himself that is entirely unambivalent. But then, unambivalent love, like perfect satisfaction, is not a creative force. Neither is perfect self-satisfaction. Too much of it and we are complacent; too little and we are insecure. A self is always teetering in that balance. It never stops being subject to anxiety. It never stops needing to give and get the sort of love that can help the feelings that underlie anxiety become tolerable, even creative. Only a rare—and perhaps not very attractive—sort of self isn't undermined or diminished by lack of love.

It is a mistake, in any case, to locate all dependence in childhood.[28] Old age (notoriously) is a second childhood—one with no future. Illness, which can strike at any time, reveals the dependence on others that is always there. A self is strong not when it is self-sufficient, but when it can acknowledge its dependence honestly and give freely because it can take without feeling compromised or diminished. The need always to be the one who gives, sometimes mistaken for generosity, is often a defense against the dependence taking would signify.

Imagine a child whose mother, instead of noticing his needs and anxieties, projects her own onto him. He is quiescent. She grows anxious. Should he be so quiet? Is there something wrong with him? Unable to contain herself, she fusses with him till he becomes active. Another scenario: She sees his nascent wishes and desires not as things to be cultivated, developed, and explored—not as opportunities to get to know him—but as levers by means of which he can be controlled and made responsive to her desires ("You can have that, but only if you do this"). In each case, her desire overrides his. In each, an opportunity is created for him to experience her love—her capacity to acknowledge and respond appropriately to his feelings and desires—as inadequate. He may then say to himself, as it were, "I cannot trust my mother's love;

therefore I will love myself." Where the mother ought to be in his love, he finds himself. Narcissism with its characteristic defenses has taken root in him.[29]

Yet, for all that, he isn't in a position to love himself successfully. He hasn't achieved the sort of autonomy his response to his mother projects. He cannot satisfy his own desires and needs or assuage his own anxieties and pains. He cannot even be confident that what he interprets as a failure in his mother isn't a failure in himself: maybe she doesn't love him because there is something wrong with him, because he is unlovable. So he continues to crave her love, as he will later crave admiration, to shore up the fragile self that is—in two ways—failing him.

To the degree that he feels his desires and anxieties without being able to do anything about them, he experiences them as threats to his own comforting fantasy of omnipotent autonomy, as things to defend himself against. Not to feel them has become a desideratum. If the defense succeeds, the place where feelings should occur in him contains only—perhaps confused—thoughts.

Narcissism is itself a liability that accompanies love. But what it gives rise to, at least in the sort of case we have imagined, is a liability that accompanies emotions more generally—namely, *hollowness*. This is the condition of Clifford Chatterley's Aunt Eva, in D. H. Lawrence's *John Thomas and Lady Jane:* "At the middle of her she had no feelings at all. She didn't even know that, at the center, anyone *could* have feelings. She thought that the core of everybody was quite hard and quite without feeling, as every crystal is centered upon a grain of cold dust. Only, of course, the way you were elaborated upon this center of nothingness mattered. It was that which established your quality." In her sixties, her husband dead for five years, Eva recognizes what this has meant for her life: "It seems to me," she says, "as if all the years I lived with him had never been real. . . . Oh, it *was* wonderful! Yet it doesn't seem any more real to me now than a cigarette one has smoked."[30]

Eva's sense of unreality is a symptom of a disconnection between her feelings and the core on which they are elaborated—a disconnection she represents as a feature of the core itself. To be jealous of someone, for example, we typically have to think something like, "He is getting love from my lover that I should be getting," or "He is a threat to the love that is rightly mine." But if that is all jealousy amounts to in us, it is *hollow*. And what makes it so is that the adult thoughts that are elements of it have come apart from the embryonic ones which should also be present. This might be because we have developed potent narcissistic defenses or learned too well to be stoical. In either case, something has gone wrong. We are inured to a certain sort of pain. But we have paid too high a price. Like Aunt Eva, we have become cut off from a source of joy and energy that life is gray and chilly without.

Yet what makes our emotions feelings rather than mere chilly adult thoughts, what makes them non-hollow, is not their involvement with something other than thought. On the contrary, it is their involvement with thought that is infantile, alimentary—thought that is either a keeping in, a pushing out, or some other such thing connected to the inner workings of our bodies. The different "feelings" that so often accompany different emotions—and seem so oddly appropriate to them—arise in part from the awareness of such inner workings. Feelings such as the emptiness of despair, or the suffusing fullness of rage, or the heat of passion.

In the concluding sentences of his autobiography, Sean O'Faolain sums up his life as follows: "I had to . . . go on writing, waiting and watching for the appearance, within me, of the theme that leads the writer into his Cave to talk to himself when young—to say: 'This is what you dreamed as a boy. There is no break, no chasm, just a larger shape, a more human, a more complex form.' . . . If once the boy within us ceases to speak to the man who enfolds him, the shape of life is broken and there is, literally, no more to be said."[31] In Aunt Eva's Cave, the girl still speaks, but nothing she says is intelligible to the enfolding woman, whose life, in consequence, seems hollow at its core.

6

SENTIMENTALITY AND THE GIFT OF THE SELF

In a well-known passage in Turgenev's *Fathers and Sons,* the idea that love is the gift of the self is connected to the idea of value, and to a sort of inverse Kantian anxiety about it:

> "Are you so disillusioned?" asked Bazarov. "No," Madam Odintsov replied, speaking with deliberation. "But I am unsatisfied. I think if I could really get attached to something . . ." "You are longing to fall in love," Bazarov interrupted her, "but you can't. That is the reason for your unhappiness." Madame Odintsov began to examine the mantilla over her sleeve. "Am I incapable of love?" she murmured. "Probably. Only I was wrong to call it unhappiness. On the contrary, the person most to be pitied is the one who meets with that experience." "What experience do you mean?" "Falling in love." "And how do

you come to know that?" "By hearsay," Bazarov retorted angrily. "You're playing the coquette," he thought to himself. "You are bored, and teasing me for want of something better to do, while I . . ." And indeed he felt his heart bursting. "Besides you may be too demanding," he said, leaning his whole body forward and playing with the fringe on his chair. "Possibly I am. I want everything or nothing. A life for a life. If you take mine, give me yours. And no regrets or turning back. Otherwise, better have nothing!" "Well," observed Bazarov, "those are fair terms, and I am surprised that so far you haven't found what you want." "And do you think it would be easy to surrender yourself completely to whatever it might be?" "Not easy, if you start deliberating, biding your time, putting a price on yourself, taking care of yourself, I mean; but to give yourself recklessly is very easy." "But how can one help valuing oneself? If I have no value, who would want my devotion?" "That is not my affair: It is for the other person to discover my value. What matters is to know how to give yourself." Madame Odintsov leaned forward from the back of her chair. "You speak as if you had experienced it all," she said. "No, words, idle words arising out of our conversation: as you know, all that is not in my line." "But would you be capable of surrendering yourself unreservedly?" "I don't know. I shouldn't like to boast."[1]

Madame Odintsov's anxiety might be put like this: If I give myself, I act as if I set no value on myself (what you value, you don't give away; what you give away, you don't value). Kant's thought, inversely, is that what you dis-value, you don't reveal. It is a form of economic thinking about love, a way of putting a price on yourself. Bazarov's reply that it is for your lover to discover your value brings to the fore a crucial tension. Love has its own logic, he implies, which the deliberating will offends. Start deliberating and you will end up unable to take the risk of loving.

It is an idea that can make us glad that sexual desire operates independently of our will, and so can initiate gifts rational prudence might not sanction. At the same time, it is too formulaic a response to love's confusions to convince fully. The self is not as much in our reckless gift as Bazarov would have us—and especially Madame Odintsov—believe. Of course, we can seem—even to ourselves—to have given, in the same way that Bazarov feels his heart bursting. We can go through the gifting motions. But whether or not we have delivered the goods isn't up to us. We may have nothing to give; what we have may not be in our gift. Bazarov may be right that it is for our lover to discover our value. But he isn't right because the value is guaranteed to be there and genuine love guaranteed to find it. It is, rather, that the right sort of anxiety-transmuting finding ensures the value—to the lover, at least—of what it finds.

In Aldous Huxley's *Eyeless in Gaza* both ideas are convincingly explored. The central character, Anthony Beavis (Benger), is a young boy in boarding school when his mother dies. His friends—awkward in the face of such an anxiety-inducing event—exclude him from the normal school life of pranks, smutty jokes, and cruelty. This brings him closer to Brian Foxe, whose stammer has also made him something of an outcast. In an overture to friendship, Brian shows Anthony a paper boat he has built, and the two agree to sail it in the gutter outside their dormitory window after lights-out. At first, the boys are deeply absorbed in the fate of the boat—a transparent allegory of their incipient relationship. Then their attention is caught by the starry heavens above, as Kant calls them:

> There was a silence. Then, with decision, as though he had at last made up his mind to have it out, at any cost, "S-sometimes," said Brian, "I w-wonder wh-whether they aren't really al-live." He looked anxiously at his companion: was Benger going to laugh? But Anthony, who was looking up at the stars, made no sound or movement of derision; only nodded gravely. Brian's shy defenceless little secret was safe, had received no wound. He felt profoundly grateful; and suddenly it was as though a great wave were mounting, mounting through his body. He was almost suffocated by that violent uprush of love and ("Oh, suppose it had been *my* mother!") of excruciating sympathy for poor Benger.

For a while Anthony can contain the thought he hasn't derided. But then the word "alive" reminds him of a hurt baby bird he had been afraid to pick up, and how his mother had made fun of him for his fear. That in turn leads him to think of his atheist Uncle James and how he would laugh at Anthony now: "Stung by this imaginary mockery and ashamed of having been betrayed into such childishness, 'But how can they be alive?' he asked resentfully, turning away from the stars. Brian winced. 'Why is he angry?' he wondered. Then aloud, 'Well,' he started, 'if G-god's alive . . .'" But Anthony is armored there: "'My uncle,' said Anthony, 'he doesn't even believe in God. I don't either,' he added provocatively."

Things might have ended at that point had Brian responded to Anthony's defensive anger with defensiveness of his own. But that isn't what happens:

> Brian did not take up the challenge. "I s-say," he broke out impulsively, "I s-say, B-b-b-. . ." The very intensity of his eagerness made his stammer all the worse. "B-benger," he brought out at last. It was an agony to feel the current of his love thus checked and diverted. Held up behind the grotesquely irrelevant impediment to its progress, the stream mounted, seemed to gather force and was at last so strong within him that, forgetting altogether that it wasn't done, Brian suddenly laid his arm on Anthony's arm. The fingers travelled down the sleeve, then closed around the bare wrist; and thereafter, every time his stammer interposed itself between his feeling and its object, his grip tightened in

a spasm almost of desperation. "I'm so t-terri-
bly sorry about your m-mother," he went on.
"I d-didn't w-want to s-say it be-before. N-not
in f-front of the others. You know, I was th-th-
th-. . ." He gripped on Anthony's wrist more
tightly; it was as though he were trying to sup-
plement his strangled words by the direct elo-
quence of touch, were trying to persuade the
other of the continued existence of the stream
within him, of its force, unabated in spite of the
temporary checking of its current. He began the
sentence again and acquired sufficient momen-
tum to take him past the barrier. "I was th-
thinking just n-now," he said, "it m-might have
been *my* mother. Oh, B-b-beavis, it m-must be
too awful!" Anthony looked at him, in the first
moment of surprise, with an expression of suspicion, almost of fear on his face. But as the
other stammered on, this first hardening of resistance melted away, and now, without feeling
ashamed of what he was doing, he began to cry.[2]

What happens between Anthony and Brian is a reciprocal gift of self. But for it to take place, much that is sheer
luck has to be present. First, Anthony's attention has to
be sufficiently absorbed by the stars that occasion its exposure for Brian's shy defenseless little secret to escape instant derision. Second, this secret has to play so special a
role in Brian's psyche that Anthony's failure to deride it
can produce a very intense gratitude. Third, Brian's love

for his own mother has to be sufficiently great to make him empathically identify with Anthony. Fourth, Brian has to stammer: it causes the force of his love to increase by opposing its too rapid expression; it allows him to overcome schoolboy taboos and touch Anthony. Finally, all this has to provide Anthony with enough security that he can finally feel the loss of his mother and mourn it without shame. The tears he sheds are his gift of himself to Brian.

In the course of the exchange, the value of Brian's stutter is revealed. In school, it has been an isolating liability, a cause of mockery. Now it is something that can melt away resistance, at least of the sort caused by a fear of being mocked as childish. Similarly, the value of Anthony's defense mechanism, occasioned by the mockery of his mother and uncle, is also—though perhaps less plainly—shown. Without it, Anthony might give himself too easily and suffer pain that would transform his defenses into a fortress.

Something else happens in Anthony and Brian, something we can best get at by imagining what might have happened to their feelings had things gone otherwise. If Brian's love had failed to overcome Anthony's resistance and had instead increased it, Brian would be less likely to love again—his confidence in the power of his love would be lessened. And Anthony . . . well, he would be that much harder to love, because in failing to overcome his fear of making himself vulnerable, he would have increased it. What their reciprocal gift does to each is to allow these emotions to develop, to grow. (Contrast the exchange between Ray and Iris Finch.)

Sentimentality, Oscar Wilde tells us in one of his deepest epigrams, is "merely the bank-holiday of cynicism." It is wanting to have "the luxury of an emotion without paying for it."[3] Since the Wildean cynic is someone "who knows the cost of everything and the value of nothing,"[4] we are clearly in Bazarovian territory—territory F. R. Leavis has insightfully explored. Discussing Alexander Smith's—now forgotten—poem "Barbara,"[5] Leavis writes:

> It has all the vices that are to be feared when his theme is proposed, the theme of irreparable loss. It doesn't merely surrender to temptation; it goes straight for a sentimental debauch, an emotional wallowing, the alleged situation being only the show of an excuse for the indulgence, which is, with a kind of innocent shamelessness, sought for its own sake. If one wants a justification for invoking the term "insincerity," one can point to the fact that the poem clearly *enjoys* its pang: to put it more strictly, the poem offers a luxurious enjoyment that, to be enjoyed, must be taken for the suffering of an unbearable sorrow. The cheapness of the sentimentality appears . . . immediately in the move-

> ment, the clichés of phrase and attitude, and
> the vaguenesses and unrealities of situation.[6]

The enjoyment of a stock feeling precisely as such (here the irreparable loss of a lover); cheapness (Wilde's idea again); the use of clichés; the fantasy-like vaguenesses and unrealities of situation—these, for Leavis, are the hallmarks of the sentimental.

The same hallmarks are present—with a revelatory illustration—in the discussion of kitsch (a form of sentimentality) that constitutes the theoretical centerpiece of Milan Kundera's novel *The Unbearable Lightness of Being*:

> The senator stopped the car in front of a stadium with an artificial skating rink, and the children jumped out and started running along the large expanse of grass surrounding it. Sitting behind the wheel and gazing dreamily after the four little bounding figures, he said . . ., "Just look at them." And describing a circle with his arm, a circle that was meant to take in stadium, grass, and children, he added, "Now that is what I call happiness." . . . How did the senator know that children meant happiness? Could he see into their souls? What if, the moment they were out of sight, three of them jumped the fourth and began beating him up? The senator had only one argument in his favor: his feeling. When the heart speaks, the mind finds it indecent to object. In the realm of kitsch, the dictatorship of the heart reigns supreme. The

feeling induced by kitsch must be a kind the multitudes can share. Kitsch may not, therefore, depend on an unusual situation; it must derive from the basic images people have engraved in their memories: the ungrateful daughter, the neglected father, children running on the grass, the motherland betrayed, first love. Kitsch causes two tears to flow in quick succession. The first tear says: How nice to see children running in the grass! The second tear says: How nice to be moved, together with all mankind, by children running in the grass! It is the second tear that makes kitsch kitsch. The brotherhood of man on earth will be possible only on a base of kitsch.[7]

What Kundera rightly recognizes is that sentimentality involves a drama in which we are both actor and audience, and where the pleasure sought requires a conventional plot. For what we seek is reassurance that we do feel what we are supposed to feel—what right-feeling people the world over feel. We play the role of the lover not because we love, but to reassure ourselves that we love—a reassurance that the pleasure we get from seeing ourselves in the role provides. But this reassurance is triangulated: between us and our feeling lies the brotherhood of man. It isn't simply the reassurance of fellow-feeling, however, but of feelings that are scripted, safe, clichéd. The theater of real love is improvisational, open ended. There's no guarantee it won't be a tragedy or won't end up costing us more in the way of pain than we can afford. The theater of sentimentalized love, by contrast, is a cul-de-sac: the children will never beat each other up.

Kundera doesn't explicitly mention sincerity, as Leavis does, but it is clearly in his picture by implication—though perhaps what we ought to call it, at least in the senator, is inauthenticity. For the senator is obviously sincere. But authentic? If authenticity requires us to be ourselves, and if to be ourselves "we must not be like anyone else," as Lionel Trilling nonapprovingly puts it, sentimentality pretty much entails inauthenticity.[8]

It is an entailment Leavis and Kundera seem to embrace. Yet a major virtue of their account of sentimentality is that it allows us to distinguish between expressing an authentic feeling in a shopworn way and using a cliché to induce the feeling of having an authentic feeling. In the grip of what is deepest, we often reach for a conventional phrase or text—one sanctioned by long use—precisely to avoid the lightness of the merely original. When people make up their own wedding vows or funeral services, we usually find ourselves wishing they had stuck to the Prayer Book. "I love you" is a clichéd expression of love. But attempts to find a more original one often fall flat. The cliché alone reassures.

Literature is a different matter. There we expect the writer "to refuse . . . the ready-made, the illusory and the spectral in the way of conceptual apparatus, and to keep his abstractions . . . fully charged with the concrete of experience and his thinking . . . unquestionably faithful to it."[9] The virtues of literature, however, are not those of life. No doubt we should all aspire to be the authors of our own lives, but we can't all expect to write master-pieces.

The gift of the self Anthony makes to Brian is the gift of his authentic grief. For all that, there is nothing partic-ularly original about its manifestation: he weeps. What matters is that the grief be his to give—that it be some-thing *he* pays for, that he suffers. But the payment must be a blank check. It can't have the price filled in. The cynic thinks the price is always filled in, that no one hands out blank checks. When, on a bank holiday, he al-lows himself to feel, what he feels always has the price tag still attached. (The banks won't be closed forever.)

When our feelings are prix fixe, our losses are illusory—as are our gains. But if life is eternal—if there is redemp-tion, restoration, an end to loss—aren't all prices fixed? Doesn't Christianity, by promising these things, senti-mentalize—hollow out—the love it is supposedly based on? The thought that it does is what makes intelligi-ble Blake's famous line, "Eternity is in love with the pro-ductions of time."[10] The Christian god needs us, so that—albeit vicariously—he can come as close as eternal beings can to really living. When, unlike the Greek gods, he offers us eternal life too, the whole game threatens to collapse.

Sentimentality as a style of cynicism is something like a global habit of mind. As such, there is little to be said in its favor. But simply as a style, as part of a wardrobe, it has advantages—as does cynicism itself. We can't be au-thentic all the time. Sometimes we have to feign or dramatize feelings. To be unable to bring ourselves to do so, as Cordelia cannot, isn't always a sign of advanced integrity. Instead, it can be a defect of love—a need to reassure ourselves that we really feel, and to do this by not acting according to people's expectations.

A diet of sentimental movies may be for the soul what a diet of candy is for the body, but because the sentimental is related to the authentic—because it is, as it were, a clichéd version of the authentic—instead of expressing a deadness within, it can stir up what was slumbering. It can help to locate muscles in our psyche—muscles that we need to exercise.

7

LEBENSRAUM, DESIRE, AND THE ENVY OF ETERNITY

When Eve Kosofsky Sedgwick was asked by her therapist what she got from her nonsexual relationship with Michael Moon she replied:

> Gee, it has changed me in a hundred big and little ways. There is so much pleasure! I've always had a lot of funniness in my life, even when I was near-suicidal, but before Michael I don't think I knew anyone who could *always* make me laugh out loud, laugh with my whole body, anytime it occurred to them to want to. Not sure I even knew what the feeling was like before. No, Michael has these big, queer, expressive talents—ventriloquism, esoterica, tells stories so they stay told; his people seem more real than real people. I never feel I've read a book until Michael has channeled it for me—really, that

> goes for my own life too. And what's rarest is
> how he uses these things to make a world, a
> kind of warm, musical, hilarious private culture
> to share with the people he loves.[1]

Michael has talents and Eve sees them. They sustain love because they help make an intimate world where new pleasures, unavailable elsewhere, are created. When you see love in this way, getting and giving seem barely distinguishable—which is one advantage, I think, of so seeing it.

The space love opens or creates for intimacy is Lebensraum—in our case, typically a house or apartment, which love transforms into a home. Making a home for itself, you might say, is love's work. But when there is war or plague or terror or economic depression or social oppression, the scope of this work is revealed. What love must do then, we see, is make not just a home, but a world. Genuine Platonic love—as opposed to what is popularly known as such, namely, aim-inhibited or asexual love—is love with its worldmaking wings spread wide.

Socrates is wise (famously) in knowing only that he knows nothing worthwhile. Yet included under that rubric is something we would all like to possess. "The only thing I say I know," he claims in the *Symposium*, "is the art of love [*ta erôtika*]."[2] Its inclusion there, initially perplexing, becomes a little less so, once we see there is a Platonic pun involved: *erôs* means "love"; *erôtan* "to ask questions." The art of love, in other words, is being identified with the Socratic art of asking questions, of midwifery—a

thought Freud will make his own. As an art of asking rather than answering, it is also one that Socrates,
though ignorant, can possess.

Hippothales expresses his love by writing encomia to
his beloved. In Socrates' view, no skilled lover would
do that. If your suit succeeds and you win the boy, fair
enough. But "if he gets away, the greater your praise of his
beauty and goodness, the more you will seem to have lost
and the more you will be ridiculed. That is why someone
who is wise in the art of love doesn't praise his beloved
until he has him: he fears how the future may turn out."[3]
Convinced, Hippothales turns to Socrates for instruction
in how to do better with his new boyfriend, Lysis—instruction Socrates is happy to provide: "If you're willing
to have him talk with me, I might be able to give you
a demonstration of how to carry on a discussion with
him."[4] What follows is a typical Socratic conversation in
which Lysis is forced to recognize his own ignorance of
what love is.

The process sounds chastening, even humiliating. But
it is something more: a step in the creation of a type of
lover—a lover of wisdom, a philosopher: "Those who are
already wise no longer love wisdom, whether they are
gods or men. Neither do those who are so ignorant that
they are bad, for no bad and stupid person loves wisdom.
There remains only those who have this bad thing, ignorance, but have not yet been made ignorant and stupid by
it. They are conscious of not knowing what they don't
know."[5] By getting Lysis to recognize that he doesn't
know, Socrates sets him on the road to loving wisdom—

the only road to true love. Love, by revealing a lack or need, creates desire. But once satisfied, that desire is dead.

Socrates is a master of foreplay, but he won't have sex with you—as Alcibiades famously learns—and can't answer the questions with which he makes you hungry. Clearly then, he needs further instruction in the erotic arts. In the *Symposium,* Plato—like a good lover—arranges to have Diotima provide him with it. What all of us love, according to her, is happiness—that is, we want good things to be ours forever. But because we are mortal, the closest we can come to satisfying this desire is "reproduction and birth in beauty."[6] In the case of heterosexual lovers, who are "pregnant in body," this consists in producing children who resemble—and so share in the beauty of—their parents. Homosexual lovers are a different story. They are "pregnant in soul," and give birth not to children, but to "wisdom and the rest of virtue." When a man who is pregnant in soul finds a beautiful boy, Diotima says, it "makes him instantly teem with stories of virtue," "beautiful stories."[7]

Though giving birth to virtue and giving birth to stories about it are obviously different, some of the other phrases Diotima uses show us how to mitigate the difference. What homosexual lovers want is to give birth to stories about virtue of a particular sort—ones that, because they can be used in "the proper ordering of cities and households," can help "make young men better."[8] Their stories, in other words, are social codes, systems of laws, and constitutions that prescribe how young men are to live and spend their time—those serious stories that in Plato's last work, the *Laws,* are referred to as tragedies: "We're tragedians ourselves, and our tragedy is the best and finest we can create. At any rate, our entire constitution has been constructed so as to be a 'representation' of the finest and noblest life—the very thing we maintain is most genuinely a tragedy."[9]

If such stories are to serve this social purpose, however, they cannot be products of distorting fantasy, as Nietzsche thinks our moral stories are, and as some feminists think our story of romantic love itself is. To ensure as far as possible that they aren't, the philosopher studies the beauty of ways of life and laws and the beauty of the sciences. What he acquires from these studies are the conceptual resources needed to see the world, including the social or political world, aright—to gain expert knowledge of it. (In Plato's view, these are the resources that put us in touch with his unchanging, intelligible Forms.)

This isn't the project we undertake when we reflect on our own love stories in hopes of understanding them better—often a project provoked by an unhappy ending. Instead, it is the project of philosophy, as Plato conceives of it—a project that culminates in "the birth of many gloriously beautiful stories in unstinting love of wisdom."[10] Yet his grander project intersects with ours. For our love stories, too, must be intelligible if they are to be coherently livable. If they aren't, a lover who tries to live them out will find himself embroiled in something he cannot understand—something whose unintelligibility Socratic questioning, or psychoanalysis, or just plain critical scrutiny may help reveal. It is this sort of incoherence, encountered at lower stages in Diotima's ladder of love, that leads the lover, under pressure from his rational love of intelligibility, to climb to the next stage.

What initially hooks him is the beauty of a particular body, understood as constituting a standard of beauty for him. That is why—later in his love-inspired journey—beauty will no longer seem to him to be "*measured by* gold or raiment or beautiful boys or youths."[11] But because his love leads him to give birth to *stories,* he inevitably comes to see his boyfriend's beautiful body as one among many: if it is beautiful, so are any other bodies the story fits. "Realizing this, he is established as a lover of all beautiful bodies and relaxes this excessive preoccupation with one, thinking less of it and believing it to be a small matter."[12]

It is important that Diotima's description of this change is comparative and contrastive: the lover used to be excessively preoccupied with his beloved; now he loves him appropriately. But loving appropriately is still loving. The boy is included in the class of those with beautiful bodies the lover now loves. It is also important that change in knowledge and change in desire accompany each other. To recognize his beloved as one among many, the lover's love for him has to develop and expand. And that means psychological resources within him—beyond his sexual responsiveness to physical beauty—must come into play. More of him must be involved in his love. So what his boyfriend loses in exclusivity, he gains in richness of response, and no doubt also in endurance and reliability of response. When his physical beauty (his bloom, as the Greeks call it) fades, he will now still be loved.

If love is to escape frustration, however, it cannot stop with bodies. If it is to be intelligible, immune to Socratic criticism, it must lead on from bodies to souls, and so to the beautiful laws and practices that improve them. This cognitive achievement is again matched by a conative one. When the lover sees all these beautiful things as somehow akin in beauty, he comes to think that "bodily beauty is a small thing," and so, as before, becomes less obsessed with it.[13]

At the top of Diotima's ladder of love lies "the beautiful itself"—the Platonic Form of beauty—which is the first loved object that isn't in any way transcended. Here the lover at last seems to find something worthy of the obsessive attention he once lavished on his boyfriend:

> You and many another are ready to gaze on those you love and dwell with them forever, if somehow it were possible, not to eat or drink but only to watch and be with them. What then do we suppose it would be like . . . if it were possible for someone to see the beautiful itself, pure, unalloyed, unmixed, not full of human flesh and colors, and the many other kinds of nonsense that attach to mortality, but if he could behold the divine beauty itself that is single in nature? Do you think it a worthless life . . . for a man to look there and contemplate *that*

> with that by which one must contemplate it,
> and to be with it? Or are you not convinced . . .
> that there alone it will befall him, in seeing the
> beautiful with that by which it is visible, to be-
> get, not an image of virtue, because he doesn't
> touch an image, but true virtue, because he
> touches what's true? But in begetting true vir-
> tue and nurturing it, it is given to him to be-
> come god-beloved, and if any other among men
> is immortal, he is too.[14]

Nonetheless, obsession is out of place even in this case:
the beautiful itself cannot satisfy the lover's thirst or
hunger any more than his boyfriend can. In its presence—
as in that of the boy—what the lover *would* do if it were
possible mustn't be confused with what he *can* and *does*
do. The lover who has reached the beautiful itself can
make good things his own forever only by giving birth in
the true beauty he has at last found. This he accom-
plishes precisely by building a social world in which his
boyfriend can grow up, become truly virtuous, and live
with him in the contemplation of that beauty. Lebensraum, in his case, is thus on a particularly grand scale.
But so, in extremis, it is in our own.

The Platonic lover's apparent abandonment of his beloved for another and better one isn't in fact abandonment. Like Odysseus, the lover leaves to return. It is simply that love's task—namely, opening up a space where
lover and beloved can do their loving—forces it to have
"shifting involvements."[15] Work, like war, takes the lover

away, and so threatens the love which motivates him to leave. Far from home, in the office or on the isle of Ogygia, lie other things to love—including very abstract things (the beautiful itself) and very tempting ones (beautiful nymphs like Calypso).

Love is a desire, Plato thinks, and desire an inanition—an emptiness of either the body (hunger, thirst) or the soul (ignorance). What fills the emptiness is what satisfies the desire, and what fills it most permanently is what provides the most robust and lasting pleasure: "If being filled with what is appropriate to our nature is pleasant, what is more filled with things that *are* more, more really and truly enjoys a more true pleasure, whereas what partakes of things that *are* less is less truly and surely filled and partakes of a less trustworthy and less true pleasure."[16] But if the emptiness is in a leaky vessel (the body) and the filling is something that decays (food), it cannot be filled once and for all: no matter how much we eat, we will be hungry again later, since the food will have been absorbed or excreted. If the emptiness is in the permanently existing soul, however, it can be permanently filled: the soul isn't leaky (it has no alimentary canal), and what it is filled with (knowledge of the truth) is immutable.

This is an immensely seductive picture, in part because it seems to resonate with the actual phenomenology of desiring. No doubt that is why it keeps finding defenders: "Once before the gods split us in two, we were complete beings. Now we are incomplete ones, condemned to love or desire the missing half that will complete us." This is the well-known story Plato puts into the mouth of Aristophanes in the *Symposium.* It is echoed in our own time by Octavio Paz ("Love is not a desire for beauty; it is a yearning for completion") and by many others.[17] "Once, before we were embodied, our souls lived with an object— the beautiful itself—which perfectly requited our love, by blissfully filling the emptiness in our souls." Cast in the conative voice, so to speak, this is Plato's story of recollection and of philosophy as a preparation for death-as-disembodiment and a return to requited bliss. (Replace "the beautiful itself" with the Christian "God" and it is Augustine's story in the *Confessions.*) "Once, before our father castrated us (or before the trauma of birth), we lived with or in an object—our mother—that perfectly requited our love": this is the Freudian account, grossly simplified. The only difference between the three is that what in Aristophanes and Plato is an emptiness or lack is, in Freud, an excitation seeking a discharge that will restore the organism to pleasant quiescence.

It is hardly surprising, then, that erotic Platonism's purist avatar is a Freudian: Jacques Lacan. Like his Platonic ancestor, Lacanian man has desire as his essence. The distinctive wrinkle is that while the relevant Platonic desire is a rational desire for wisdom, the Lacanian one is unconscious, and so—like all unconscious desire, in Lacan's view—sexual. But that difference aside, the accounts are parallel. "Desire is a relation of being to lack," Lacan writes. "The lack is the lack of being, properly speaking. It isn't the lack of this or that, but lack of being whereby the being exists."[18] We exist as desiring, because we aren't completely filled-in beings—because something is missing.

In Lacanian psychoanalysis, unconscious desire acquires an account: "That the subject should come to recognize and to name his desire: that is the efficacious action of analysis."[19] But because the unconscious is precisely what cannot be known, cannot be fully put into words, no account can ever capture an unconscious desire or what it is for. (Embryonic concepts have no exact adult equivalents.) There is always something left over, which Lacan calls *objet petit a,* or "object small *a.*"

Though *objet petit a* can never be possessed, its Platonic analogue can. When an irrefutable account of beauty is augmented or replaced by contemplation of the Form of beauty, love is fully satisfied and our emptiness is filled once and for all. This is the first manifestation of the deep problem in Platonic love. We desire only what we do not possess (a view Proust also adopts, as we have seen). But the pleasure of complete possession kills desire and with it the incomplete being whose essence it is. Love requited is death. That Plato's love-gift to the ever erotic Socrates should turn into its opposite in this way is an irony we can imagine Socrates himself relishing.

"Being," for Plato and Lacan, functions as a noun that names a complete, wholly present object or state. For Aristotle, it functions as a verb. And this grammatical or conceptual switch leads to an apparently very different picture of desire. What we all desire, at least if we are wise, Aristotle claims, is to live well—an activity, not an object.

The various objects we desire, we desire as contributors to it. We do not want to possess them in some mere empti-ness-filling way, with each assigned its own form-fitting psychic niche; rather, we wish to use or employ or enjoy in some way that enhances life. The desire to live well is sat-isfied in living well. But it isn't an emptiness that living well fills and kills. It is an emptiness that living well goes on filling, and so keeps active.

On the surface, this is a more appealing picture than Plato's. Yet it, too, embodies a fundamental Platonic error: the envy of eternity. If only, Plato fantasizes, we weren't moving shadows, but the unmoving, unchanging casters of shadows. If only "being" were a noun instead of a verb. Never mind, Aristotle responds; though it is a verb, in its paradigmatic or focal connotation, it might as well be a noun. For being, in that sense, is an activity *(energeia)* not a process *(kinêsis)*. Consider: Building a house is a process. At each moment you are doing it, you haven't done it yet. So at each moment it is incomplete. Moreover, it is something that must end: once you have built your house, your building it is over, finished. Con-trast that with living well. It is an activity, because at each moment you both are living well and have done so. More-over, there is nothing in the nature of living well to stop you from going on living well eternally. At each moment living well is complete, and there need be no end to such moments. Activities are thus full presences just like Pla-tonic beings. Yet they can go on forever. That is why Aris-totle's god, as the best of the beings, is an activity.[20]

When Enobarbus describes Cleopatra as making "hun-gry where most she satisfies," he semi-Aristotelianizes her.[21] But there is at least a suggestion in his formula of something else: the emptiness Cleopatra completely fills, she thereby expands. And it is that possibility which uncovers Aristotle's envy. A Platonic being eternally fills desire but kills it in the process. An Aristotelian activity fills desire at each moment, can go on doing so eternally, and so keeps it active, unkilled. Yet it still arrests desire's development, keeping it locked in an obsessive—though perhaps satisfyingly—unchanging pattern. Arrested development may be okay for a god, who has no developing to do, but it isn't something a mere mortal should too readily embrace.

A desire not satisfied eternally—once and for all—can still be satisfied for now. A good dinner satisfies our hunger, even though we will be hungry again. With luck, this means there will be new satisfactions in the future, even for old desires. Our desires are many and various, in any case. When one is satisfied or frustrated, there is usually another. And even if there isn't, old ones are educable and expansible: what satisfies the appetite of a neophyte won't work on that of a gourmand. Besides, our desire set isn't closed. New desires are constantly being added, old ones removed. The world sees to that. The enemy of desire isn't intrinsic to it or metaphysical; it is extrinsic, historical, and contingent—something about us, about our historical circumstances, and the space our love has opened.

Plato's picture of desire as an emptiness figures the ideal beloved as an object that completes the lover by perfectly filling him out. To that extent, it focuses love squarely on the beloved. At the same time, however, it suggests that all we want to do with a beloved is possess her, take her into ourselves, make her part of us. Proust writes: "Whenever the idea of women who are different from us penetrates our minds . . . we know no rest until we have converted this alien into something that is compatible with ourselves, the mind being in this respect endowed with the same kind of reaction and activity as our physical organism, which cannot abide the infusion of any foreign body into its veins without at once trying to digest and assimilate it."[22] Proust is describing the inevitable form of adult love—but we are reminded of the infant, whose love for his mother is quite literally of this form. The result is what we might call the appetitization of desire, which isn't so much a misrepresentation of it as a partly correct representation of an early stage in its potential development—"the chrysalis," as Richard Wollheim calls it, "out of which other kinds of human desire break free."[23]

One sign that love, in particular, has broken free is that the scenarios in which the beloved is involved gain in richness and open-endedness: we want not simply to possess or incorporate her (whatever that might mean in practice, as opposed to fantasy), but rather to engage with her in a variety of activities, including that of creating a space that facilitates the occurrence and invention of other activities we could not readily specify in advance. Among these will be sexual—often reproductive—activities. The space it is love's work to create is only superficially dyadic or binary. It must have room for our beloved, but also (typically) for children.

Few will agree with Plato that children are a second-best to philosophy—that everyone would rather give birth to immortal philosophical stories than to mere mortal offspring. Still, the envy of immortality has here paid a small dividend to counterbalance somewhat its considerable costs. It leads Plato to see, for instance, that reproduction is not the only—or even the privileged—creative activity available to lovers. Giving birth to stories, too, is a cooperative enterprise. When it goes well, the expansion and enrichment it brings about in the lovers' desire, not just for each other but for other things, leads to more and more of their values becoming shared or coordinated. The contribution it thereby makes to the harmony and well-functioning of their home might be seen if not as a better alternative to successful child rearing, then at least as a precondition for it. To that extent, modern couples, whose relationship is based primarily on so-called disclosing intimacy, are one of Plato's less well-recognized heirs.

We already use crude methods—dieting, exercise, orthodontia, cosmetic surgery—to transform ourselves and our children into people we think we can love, or love better. So even if love isn't responsive to value, it aspires to be a creator of it, to give birth in (what it takes to be) beauty. Soon we will be able to manipulate genes to produce yet more dramatic changes—changes that could, as it were, reconfigure the infant, at one end of life, and greatly postpone death, at the other. Love might then really conquer all. No death any more, no violence, no pain and suffering, just "a final goodbye to wars and ideologies" and "a billion balconies facing the sun."[24]

To this utopian vision, one of John Keats's letters provides a compelling antidote:

> Call the world if you Please "The vale of Soul-making." . . . I say *"Soul making"* Soul as distinguished from an Intelligence—There may be intelligences . . . in millions—but they are not Souls till they acquire identities, till each one is personally itself. . . . How then are Souls to be made? . . . How, but by the medium of a world like this? . . . By three grand materials acting the one upon the other for a series of years—These three materials are the *Intelligence*—the *human heart* (as distinguished from intelligence or Mind) and the *World* or *Elemental space* suited for the proper action of *Mind and Heart* on each other for the purpose of forming the *Soul or Intelligence destined to possess the sense of Identity.* . . . Do you not see how necessary a world of pain and troubles is to school an Intelligence and make it a soul? A Place where the heart must feel and suffer in a thousand diverse ways! . . . The Heart . . . is the teat from which the Mind or intelligence sucks its identity—As various as the Lives of Men are—so various become their souls, and thus does God make individual beings, Souls. . . . This appears to me a faint sketch of a system of Salvation which doesn't affront our reason and humanity.[25]

If Keats is right, individuals cannot be cloned as pennies are minted. Each must be individually forged in a crucible of pain and troubles. Even God couldn't make them any other way—and neither could genetic engineering.

It is a troubling thought—so troubling that Keats himself is unable to think it to the dregs. He can accept pain and troubles, but only because he sees them as compatible with salvation. It is as if once a self has been forged, once its structure established, it *is* like a penny. There is its structure, right there. Anything that has it must be that self. It took suffering to make it. But now that it is made, its suffering can end. It couldn't have been born in Heaven, but it can go live there eventually.

In the small word "live" lies the worm in this apple. Living systems, biologists tell us, must have the properties of multiplication, heredity, and variation that enable them to evolve by natural selection so as to become better adapted to their environments. Many nonliving systems are also adaptive, of course; thermostats adapt to reflect the ambient temperature. But the ones that are alive have a nearly limitless capacity to produce novel solutions to the unpredictable problems of surviving, reproducing, and flourishing that their environments present. In the terminology introduced by Mark Bedau, they are *supply adaptive.*[26]

True, the Heavenly environment never really changes, so that once a person has adapted to it (worries about monotony and boredom aside) there is no more adapting to do. But Keats can take little comfort in that. For the inner environment—inseparable from self-consciousness—does change. In vital engagement with our memories, wishes, and fantasies, in interminable self-analysis, our old selves, like old members of a species, die and new ones, through pains and troubles as intense as any, are forged to replace them.

What Heaven would arouse in such a self wouldn't for long be joy and gratitude, therefore, but a sense of deprivation, a hard-won recognition that

> The greatest poverty is not to live
> In a physical world, to feel that one's desire
> Is too difficult to tell from despair.[27]

Pain, suffering, conflict, violence, death itself—all we think we would be better off without—we would then come to see as essential not just to our creation, but to our continued (but finite) life.

Our lives contain much that is tragic (we will lose everything we love, even our dear selves) and much too, luckily, that is funny and joyful. But tragedy shouldn't be confused—as it often is in sentimental cultures like ours—with what Cornelius Castoriadis calls false tragedy:

> Should I follow this chimera of wanting to
> eliminate the tragic side of human existence? It
> seems to me that instead I want to eliminate the
> melodramatic aspect, the false tragedy—the one
> in which catastrophe arrives without necessity,
> in which everything could have been otherwise
> if only the characters had known this or had
> done that. . . . I would like an end to Guignol
> and to the transformation of people into pup-

pets of other puppets who "govern" them. When a neurotic repeats for the fourteenth time the same behavior-pattern of failure, reproducing for himself and for those nearby the same type of misfortune, helping this person to get out of such a situation is to rid his or her life of grotesque farce, not tragedy; it is to allow the person finally to see the real problems of life and the tragic element they may contain—which the neurosis served in part to express but especially to *mask.*[28]

It is the existence of false tragedy, nonetheless, that shows what else is wrong with Keats's representation of his vision as a system of salvation. Beyond the true tragedies that even God cannot eliminate from our lives, there are the false ones that he could, but doesn't. There is too much evil around, in other words, for even a Keatsian to render its existence compatible with that of an omniscient, omnipotent, omni-benevolent god.

Anxieties of loss generate fantasies of restoration, whether what we lose is our loved life or our loved lover. In Heaven, we will live forever and so will our loved ones. But that would be a dubious blessing, if they could cease to love us even there. In the literature of sadomasochism, there is a subgenre where the master encloses his beloved slave in a suit of immobilizing latex as in a living tomb, and then uses pleasure and pain to control the mind within. Imprisoned thus, she will do and feel exactly what he wants. It is a sort of death-in-life existence that makes death itself pale by comparison. (It is not much of a life for the master either, frankly. But busy assuaging his anxiety of loss, he doesn't seem to notice. He just starts over on another slave.) In Heaven, our loved ones are condemned to an essentially similar fate, since to assuage our erotic anxieties, their minds and feelings must remain unchanging.

Even if what ensures this is a pleasure so intense that no mind could ever give it up, as the pleasure of living in God's presence is alleged to be—even if, unlike in the sadomasochism stories, we are all in the same boat—something has still gone horribly awry. The anxious confusions love engenders have ended up destroying both it and its object, and Eros and Thanatos have become literally indistinguishable. "Pleasure," as Baudelaire says, "is a merciless executioner."[29]

The ineliminability of death, as of true tragedy, is difficult to accept. Even if—aided by Keats—we recognize that death-as-the-enemy-of-individual-life is a hobgoblin, there are caves in all of us where its shadow still terrifies. It haunts religious fantasies of eternal life, but also scientific ones of progress and self-salvation which reject religion altogether. Like Unamuno, we neither want to die nor do we "want to want to die." But that means we can't want "to live for ever and ever and ever" either.[30] Bernard Williams is wrong, I think, to describe the slogan "¡Viva la Muerte!" as obscene.[31] Properly understood, it is one we must all learn at least to whisper.

8

VIOLENCE, PORNOGRAPHY, AND SADOMASOCHISM

When a mother and child are together, psychologist Carol Gilligan claims, they fall naturally into "the rhythm of relationship."[1] They move in and out of contact, finding and losing and refinding each other. In the process, the child experiences the "pleasure of moving in synchrony with another person"—a pleasure that will become for her "a marker, a compass pointing to emotional true north" later on.[2] At the same time, she begins to acquire the skills of a lover, which involve being able to sense changes in those who are emotionally weaker, to tune in to the rhythms and turns of another's thoughts and feelings. It is these skills which, retained and developed, will enable her to enter into a confiding relationship, where the sort of pleasure she experienced with her mother becomes available once more.

In patriarchal societies like ours, a boy's fate is different. He is separated from his mother and deprived of intimacy with her much earlier. So he is less likely than a girl to retain and develop these harmonizing skills. In Gilligan's view, even Freud's Oedipus complex is best seen as just one of a number of devices employed to effect this mother-son separation, "sexualizing the intimacy, placing it under taboo, linking freedom with leaving women and going off with men, and making any woman who resists this separation a virtual Jocasta."[3] Once a five-year-old boy has left his mother, therefore, he is faced with a poignant dilemma. Either he must learn to hide the tender feelings and vulnerabilities he previously revealed to her, or the other boys will bully and shame him, calling him a sissy, a mommy's boy, a faggot, a pussy. Eventually, to become one of them, he hides his feelings so well even he can't find them.

When he grows up and falls in love, what was an advantage in the schoolyard becomes a liability at home. What should be an opening into relationship is blocked by anxiety: if he reveals parts of himself deemed unmanly, he will "sacrifice the love and intimacy he desires so intensely."[4] He can't even listen to his wife and daughter "without fearing that he will lose his manhood."[5] Which is too bad, because, if Gilligan is right, they know something he doesn't, something that could help him get what he wants.

As a result of their longer relationship with their mothers, girls more readily remember the pleasure it provided —a pleasure they miss in their marriages and other supposedly intimate relationships with men. Consequently, they are better able to recognize the difference between "presence and absence, between love and not love"—provided they trust their own intuitions and don't get cowed into doubting them.[6] As patriarchy's power wanes, this trust comes more easily and is harder to undermine, so that women more and more resist "the invitation to absent themselves from relationship in the name of love" and the "death-in-life existence" which comes from accepting it.[7]

Gilligan's picture of modern love is simple and bleak. It is also—oddly—lopsided, entirely ignoring work's decisive influence on the men and women her stories describe. Yet love needs work to earn its living—as it needs soldiers and police to protect it—and must shape lovers accordingly. The world for which it must shape them, moreover, is a fiercely competitive one. But it isn't that way because men run it, or because testosterone makes people aggressive: retro viruses aren't into harmonious coexistence, any more than the next-door factory, or the next-door country, or the player on the other side of the tennis net. The traits that men have traditionally developed to cope with competition may not serve them well at home, but this doesn't mean that others would serve them equally well at work.

Like Odysseus, we make sense of ourselves as subjects of narratives. Our identity is in part the identity "presupposed by the unity of the character which the unity of a narrative requires."[8] In narratological terms, patriarchy functions as a sort of master trope, so to speak—a constraint on the plots of love stories. As it loses its power, the stories it constrains become unintelligible, surd. If we try to live them out, we can't make sense of ourselves or our love lives. Gilligan ably drives home this point by revealing one sort of tragedy to which such stories seem prone: that of emotionally intact women seeking confiding intimacy with emotionally unavailable men. But she ignores the fact that in the larger world into which such stories must be knit, emotional unavailability may also be a strength. As a result, her claim that the "key to psychological and cultural transformation" lies in changing the patriarchal love story has an air of fantasy about it, suggesting—if only by omission—that the world will so readily accommodate such changes that it can safely be ignored.[9] When the terrorists with the Uzis show up, the omission is likely to prove telling.

Men's commitments have always been divided between work and home—with war or the threat of war always at least in the background. But, increasingly, women's commitments are similarly divided. When boys and girls both spend less time with a mother who also works (maybe in the military or the police) and more with a father who also takes care of them, no one knows what the effect will be on love stories or on the emotional availability of those who try to live them out.

As a twelve-year-old boy, Walter Herbert read the description of a violent sex scene in Mickey Spillane's *One Lonely Night*, involving a naked woman, a man in a trench coat, and a leather belt. His response was "a compound of sexual arousal and dread" that caused him to lose contact with his surroundings.[10] Over the years, he sought an explanation of pornography's powerful impact. Pornography is "magic, with an inherent hypnotic power." No. It victimizes its consumers by "pouring a contaminant into their otherwise robust minds, and causes actual violence against women in much the same way." No. Herbert's reaction to it was "a healthy impulse twisted by neurotic self-loathing," because of "the religious guilt pervading southern culture." No, that too was mistaken. The real explanation, when it came, was more subtle—and more pleasingly literary (Herbert is a professor of literature). "Looking back," he writes, "I can see that my experience of terrorized sexual arousal resembled that of the woman, even though the narrative placed me in the standpoint of the male aggressor. It invited me to share the snug bodily containment of the man in the belted trench coat, to become the poised ravisher holding the belt, who pauses to watch his victim tremble. Yet as the rush swept over me, I felt as though some assailant had left me gasping and abject. The scene depicted a panic that had dimly audible echoes in myself, even as I took the role of the male attacker."[11] Herbert's leitmotif is now established. *This* is how violent pornography always operates.

And the dimly audible echoes? In essence, they were produced by the mechanisms Gilligan describes: "Boy babies . . . are more emotionally expressive than girls; they show delight and irritation more readily, and they cry more. But boys are trained through systematic shaming and rebuffs to bottle up their distresses and their joys, and by the age of six they are far more inhibited than their emotionally more confident sisters."[12] The result is Terrence Real's "covert depression," an auto-immune disease that splits the male self into a manly element, fantasized as having self-reliance and self-command, and an unmanly one subject to a tenderness and compassion which threaten it.[13] The cries of this tender and compassionate element are what Herbert came to think he dimly heard as he read Spillane.

For a self thus divided, the powerful onset of sexual desire is experienced as a threat to masculine self-command and self-respect. As a result, it is attacked "not with biological agents but with psychic weapons custom-tailored for the occasion—abhorrence, ridicule, contempt, and loathing."[14] Then the male self is ready to take the pornographic step. It projects the unacknowledged unmanly realities of male experience onto women: "The canonical female victim—frightened and sexually aroused—is made to embody male experiences. She is a mirror that reflects a male predicament back into male eyes as though that predicament belongs to a woman rather than a man. The pornographic script empties women of their womanly qualities and replaces them with male qualities that men do not recognize as their own."[15] Once the hated male qualities are projected, the woman then becomes the target of the violence previously directed inward.

About the qualities women are emptied of, Herbert says little. But by implication they are quite different from the male ones pornography puts in their place. Herbertian women, like Gilliganian ones, seem fated, then, to be filled with sugar and spice till men come along with their snips and snails. But that isn't quite Herbert's view:

> The "feminine" is like music in a man's mind, distinctively man-music; but he cannot grasp it, cannot hum it to himself without losing track of it. If he is to enjoy it, women have to sing it for him, and his pleasure includes the satisfaction of thinking it is their music, not his. The "masculine" perhaps plays a comparable role in women's lives, voicing capacities that women have been socialized to deny in themselves. The mysterious processes by which personhoods are woven together through mutual projections— men and women finding their deepest selves in one another—are not always pernicious.[16]

The conclusion seems right. But Herbert doesn't seem entitled to it. For if the "masculine" is as he portrays it, what could women hope to gain from weaving it into their deepest selves besides an auto-immune disease?

Herbert is on more self-consistent ground, at least, in claiming that we need to "repudiate the manhood that dooms us to pornographic enchantments and cripples our capacity for egalitarian intimacy with women," since presumably that repudiation would also have to take place inside infected women.[17] Yet it seems an odd recommendation for him to make, even so. By his own admission, pornography taught him something very important about himself: "My investment in the scenario of pornographic violence also expressed a yearning for self-knowledge. I unconsciously wanted to reclaim as my own the feelings that were portrayed by the aroused and terrified woman, so that I perceived in the fantasy, albeit dimly, the promise of a larger acquaintance with my own life."[18] But if pornography can do that for Herbert, it could surely provide someone else with self-knowledge of a different sort.

Witness Sally Tisdale:

> The other night I was watching a film called *Images of Desire:* a naked woman, blindfolded, strapped to a chair by her ankles and wrists, expressionless, seen through bars. There is a thwack-thwack sound, and she is being circled slowly by two men, one blond-Nordic type, one swarthy-Arab type, dressed in dark leather uniforms, playing with police batons. The setup, the subsequent action, the woman's steady, expressionless silence, the soft, seductive commands of the men—I *like* that fantasy. But I don't like this, and it took me a while to identify the two problems—the uniforms and the way they hit the batons into their hands. For someone else, that *is* the juice; for me, the opposite, and the "why" there is one thing I want to understand. . . . Pornography is a story we tell about ourselves—and maybe the only, or most revealing, way to tell certain secrets.[19]

Pornography, therefore, isn't restricted any more than any other sort of story to teaching us only one lesson.

What turns us on, like what disgusts us, can show us something very detailed and particular about who we erotically are.

When women enjoy more of the egalitarian intimacy that Herbert describes, a significant part of what they will enjoy is an opportunity to explore their sexual wishes in their own ways. Herbert's tacit assumption that these ways won't include violently pornographic ones seems to be little more than a tribute that (imagined) vice is paying to (imagined) virtue. In *Hard Core,* an extraordinary study of pornographic movies, Linda Williams rightly rejects this tribute as just another symptom of male dominance:

> As I persisted in exploring specifically porno-
> graphic discourses from a feminist perspective,
> and as I probed the sexual politics of works usu-
> ally viewed as inimical to women, I began to
> see that the more discourses of sexuality there
> are, the more the hierarchies governing such
> oppositions as male/female, sadist/masochist,
> active/passive, and subject/object tend to break
> down. As long as sexual pleasure is viewed as
> having a proper function and an end—whether
> that end be reproduction, love, control over an-
> other, or even orgasm considered as a climactic
> goal-driven release—it tends to reside within the
> relatively parsimonious masculine economy of
> production. But when sexual pleasure begins to
> cultivate (already inherent) qualities of perver-
> sion; when it dispenses with strictly biological

and social functions and becomes an end in itself; when it ceases to rely on release, discharge,
or spending for fulfillment; when a desiring
subject can take up one object and then another
without investing absolute value in that object;
and finally, when this subject sees its object
more as exchange value in an endless play of
substitution than as use value for possession—
then we are in the realm of what must now be
described as a more feminine economy of consumption, an economy best represented by that
image which Steven Marcus found so disturb-
ing: the orgasmic woman masturbating "with
the aid of a mechanical-electrical instrument."[20]

Herbert abhors the fact that men fill women with their
alienated and despised desires. Yet by emptying them of
sexual desires of their own—desires that might, like
men's, find expression and articulation in violent pornography—Herbert himself creates the emptiness that
must then be filled. Surely men sometimes do imagine, as
he claims, that they are giving a woman what she really
wants by raping her. But to imagine it, they must first
have erased her desire for something else—or prevented
her from finding a way to give it effective expression. For
the "bad girl" to be within, the "good girl" must first be
constructed to contain her. In a Lacan-inspired riff, Lawrence Kramer makes this same point in more freighted
and frantic terms: "The phallus stands in a relation of

complementarity, not to another object, but to a site or bearing, the feminine position. That position exists in order to display a lack that can be made good: a fillable lack, the lack filled by the phallus, the lack by which the phallus imagines itself to be called into being, whereas (but this is a secret) the summons really goes the other way, the phallus calls the lack into being in order to imagine the lack as a call, a call for help, for closure, for rescue. The phallus calls the lack into being in order to become the phallus."[21]

In Herbert's schematic genealogy of pornographic masculinity, warriors and their initiation rites led to citizen soldiers, and these to competitive individuals engaged in the economic equivalent of war. When change to mass warfare and the corporate economy made the individual warrior ideal obsolete, however, it gave rise to "widespread sentiments of alienation"—sentiments which in turn found expression in violently transgressive conceptions of manhood.[22] The only way to escape "the prison air of other people's habits, other people's defeats, boredom, quiet desperation, and muted icy self-destroying rage," writes Norman Mailer (who serves as Herbert's representative here), is "to divorce oneself from society, to exist without roots . . . to encourage the psychopath in oneself."[23] For such men, Hebert argues, sexual violence and rape became pornographically redemptive.

The idea that the individual warrior ideal is obsolete has become a commonplace: "Even in the new age of warfare we cling to the outdated notion of the single hero able to carry out daring feats of courage on the battlefield. Such heroism is about as relevant as mounting bayonet or cavalry charges. But peddling the myth of heroism is essential, maybe even more so now, to entice soldiers into war. Men in modern warfare are in service to technology."[24] It is a message to make the warriors in the IRA, the PLO, and Al Qaeda smile their grim smiles. In the unconventional theaters of war they favor, the warrior ideal seems anything but outdated. The same might be said, indeed, about the world of work as we shall see Richard Sennett describe it.

Herbert's wish to claim as his own the feelings portrayed by Spillane's aroused and terrified woman may be touching in its way. But his treatment of the feelings of the man-in-the-trench-coat element in himself seems to manifest the very sort of sexual violence that makes that element seem worthy only of repudiation. He recognizes that "self-possession in the face of disorienting pain is incontestably a desirable trait," that being disconnected from "one's emotional vulnerabilities and those of others 'renders one a formidable soldier in any theater of combat.'"[25] Yet he sees nothing to love or admire in the men—and, increasingly, women—who cultivate these traits, so as to be able to go down the mean streets for us or fight our wars. What has happened, it seems, is that his own sexual response to violence has blinded him to its terrible beauties, and left him incapable of claiming the part of himself that he sees as its potential source. From love's space—including self-love's space—Herbert wishes violent men gone. But Ares and Aphrodite are illicit lovers. Love, though she may hate war, loves the warrior who puts his life on the line to defend her.

A warrior must be able to do irreparable damage to the body of another and risk having his own irreparably damaged. He must be capable of violence and familiar with it. At the same time, he must be gentle toward his friends and loved ones. Plato was already aware of the problem these conflicting demands impose: "Where," he writes, "are we to find a character that is both gentle and capable of great anger at the same time? After all, a gentle nature is the opposite of an angry one."[26] When Homer, in the opening line of the *Iliad*, asks the goddess to "sing Achilles' rage," a large part of what he is asking her to do is explore this opposition, its sources and consequences.

Anger or rage, in Aristotle's well-known definition, involves "a desire, accompanied by pain, to take what is believed to be revenge for what is believed to be an insult."[27] Since someone is insulted when the treatment he receives is worse than what he thinks his worth entitles him to, honored when he is given treatment proportional to what he takes his worth to be, anger is connected to worth *(aretê)* and honor *(timê)*. The bond of mutual honoring is thus a major ingredient of the emotional glue that binds warriors together. But the bond also has another side, which insult reveals. When a warrior's friend is insulted, so is the warrior himself. When Paris steals Helen, he insults Menelaus. But he also insults Agamemnon and his other friends and allies. His action says in effect: "I have nothing to fear from people like you and those who will come to your aid."

Warriors with developed senses of honor obviously make dangerous enemies. They also make uncertain friends. "Our anger," Aristotle claims, "is roused more against comrades and friends we think have insulted us than against strangers."[28] This is the tension Homer detects at the heart of the psychology of the warrior. It is the reason the goddess, when she accepts his invitation, sings about an anger directed first against Achilles' friends, then against his enemies.

The greater Achilles is, the greater the distance between his worth and the worth Agamemnon accords him when —ironically violating the very norms he is in Troy to uphold—he takes away his woman and war-prize, Briseis. The greater that distance, the greater the insult. So we shouldn't expect Achilles to be easily propitiated or won over. And he isn't. Angry at Agamemnon's insult, he withdraws from battle, with the result that his fellow Greeks die like proverbial flies.

Eventually, Achilles' best friend, Patroclus, can stand it no longer. Let me, he says to Achilles, wear your armor and fight in your place. When Achilles consents, it is a measure of his concern. Yet when honor returns to the forefront of his mind, friends tend to get upstaged. "Win me my honor," he says to Patroclus as he sends him into battle,

> my glory and my honor
> From all the Greeks, and, as their restitution,
> The girl Briseis, and many other gifts.

But once you've driven the Trojans from the ships,
You come back, no matter how much
Hera's thundering husband lets you win.
Any success you have against the Trojans
Will be at the expense of my honor.[29]

Later, however, when he hears of Patroclus' death, honor recedes in significance and friendship once again comes powerfully to the fore:

> He died
> Far from home, and he needed me to protect him.
> But now, since I'm not going home, and wasn't
> A light for Patroclus or any of the rest
> Of my friends . . .
> I'm going now to find the man who destroyed
> My beloved—Hector.[30]

Like us, Achilles has many values, which don't all fit together tidily. Under the influence of powerful feelings based on some of what he cares about, he forgets that he cares about other things too. Like us, he has much to be true to, which means that he is sometimes false to his very greatest loves. This would be a flaw, I suppose, if there were a better alternative, or if it weren't so obviously the human lot.

After Patroclus' death, Achilles becomes a terrifying instrument of destruction. We are horrified by him and his apparently bestial treatment of those he slaughters. Yet instead of simple horror, what the poem invites us to feel is the related emotion of *awe*, which is appropriate not to the merely bestial, but to the sublime—to something "in comparison with which," as Kant puts it, "everything else is small."[31] Some elements in the invitation are obvious: Achilles is the son of a goddess; he fights against gods (the river Scamander); he wears immortal armor made for him by the god Hephaestus; he is carried into battle by divine horses; Athena guides his actions. Others are somewhat harder to see. "Do you think," Zeus asks Hera, that

> if you were to enter Troy's gates,
> Get inside its long walls, and chew up Priam
> And Priam's children raw, and the rest of the Trojans,
> You might find some relief from this livid hate?[32]

The question is rhetorical. Zeus recognizes that Hera's preeminent worth justifies even so savage a reprisal as wholesale cannibalistic slaughter. That is why, in the end, he tells her to do as she pleases. (Compare the Yahweh-ordained massacres at Jericho, Ai, and Hazor, and the way the New Testament God imposes infinite punishments in Hell for finite crimes.)[33] It is against this divine template that Achilles' pitiless treatment of the Trojans he so brutally kills is intended to be seen. "Don't whine to me about my parents, You dog!" he says to Hector before he kills him:

> I wish my stomach would let me
> Cut your flesh in strips and eat it raw
> For what you've done to me.[34]

The qualities that initially strike us as simply bestial, then, in fact reveal how much like a god—how transcendently excellent—Achilles really is. Awful, indeed; but not simply horrible. Each dead Trojan is a measure of Achilles' love for Patroclus, and the enormity of the loss he feels.

Priam's demeanor as he begs for Hector's corpse moves Achilles profoundly, as it does all of Homer's readers: "I have gone through what no other mortal on earth has gone through; I have put my lips to the hands of the man who has killed my children."[35] But Achilles' anger remains a threatening presence despite it. "Don't provoke me," he says,

> Stop stirring up anger in my heart,
> Or I might not let you out of here alive, old man—
> Suppliant though you are—and sin against Zeus.[36]

Motives remain mixed, values many, and tomorrow Achilles will be back on the battlefield winning honor by slaughtering Trojans.

At the outset of the *Iliad*, Achilles is a pious man able to restrain his anger when asked to do so by Athena. At its end, he is no different. He hasn't permanently learned some important moral lesson or become a changed man, less prone to anger. The costs of being a great warrior have simply been set beside its glories. To think one could have the glories without the costs is to think against Homer. It is to flee the intense sunlight of the *Iliad* for the twilight of redemptive fantasy.

In the world of Achilles, the two urns at the doorsill of Zeus—one filled with good things for us, the other with evil—are permanent fixtures. There is no final triumph of good, no heavenly reward or hellish punishment. Peace is a transient but recurring achievement; war, a recurring but transient horror. Force indeed "makes a thing of anybody who comes under its sway,"[37] but it can also "exalt someone subjected to it into a martyr or a hero."[38] Warrior excellence is a two-edged sword, sublime and terrible, like beauty in Helen or sexual attractiveness in Paris. The god in Achilles that makes him great is "part and parcel of the God that cries *Revenge!*" when he is wronged.[39]

Unlike war, where the sex is largely sublimated and the violence real, sadomasochism (s/m) is a form of consensual theater, where the sex is real but the violence is scripted by the contract that the "top" (master) and "bottom" (slave) sign ahead of time. That is why s/m is a tale of two masochists. For the true sadist's pleasure, as Octavio Paz notes, is "dulled if he realizes that his victim is also his accomplice."[40] But precisely because Paz is right, Michel Foucault is also right to reject the suggestion that s/m and true sadism are somehow in cahoots. "The idea that s/m is related to deep violence, that s/m practice is a way of liberating this violence, this aggression, is stupid. We know very well what all these people are doing is not aggressive; they are inventing new possibilities of pleasure with strange parts of their body—through the eroticization of the body."[41]

Though s/m focuses on the familiar sites of infantile sexuality, Foucault argues that it has "as one of its main features . . . the *desexualization* of pleasure."[42] What makes his argument intelligible is the conception of sex it presupposes: ejaculatory sex in a context of male dominance. Pleasure is desexualized, then, when it is dissociated from this. Whether it can be, and whether in s/m it is, are surely important matters. But equally important is another that Foucault himself also raises: "Sexuality is something that we ourselves create. . . . We have to understand that with our desires, through our desires, go new forms of relationships, new forms of love, new forms of creation. Sex is not a fatality: it's a possibility for creative life."[43] So the issue for s/m isn't simply whether it can be dissociated from phallocentrism and male dominance, but whether it is indeed such a possibility.

Just as "no comparably influential literary form is so pervasively a matter of conventions" as the Gothic, no comparably influential sexuality is as scripted as s/m.[44] When we visit our local dominatrix or look at the drawings of Tom of Finland, we see how narrow its imaginative field actually is. So if creativity is the issue, s/m seems compromised. But it isn't the issue. For what is distinctive about s/m is that it allows us to flirt with powerful forces we can't control in a reassuringly controlled—because negotiated—way. And what makes this possible, in turn, is precisely s/m's lack of creativity, its scriptedness. The pain that in other contexts can always get out of hand won't in this one, since there is always our safeword. Bound and gagged, we get a vivid illusion of what it means to be a prisoner, with our life in someone else's hands. Released, we get an equally vivid illusion of freedom's joys. We have encountered Eros and Thanatos and escaped alive.

While the need for a script reveals the need for safety, it

also brands s/m as sentimental. But because the pain produced and experienced is indubitably real, there is an attractive bonus: the other feelings involved also take on an aura of indubitable reality. When effects so potent are to be had so cheaply, lack of creativity may seem a small matter.

Though s/m is just theater, it tends to provoke extreme reactions—even in those who should know better. Mark Edmundson, for example, worries about the effect of s/m on its practitioners. "I suspect," he writes, "that often what begins in sophisticated farce ends in an intensity and maybe too a passion that is closer to tragic."[45] A groundless worry, if statistics and not revulsion is to be our guide. Then he worries about s/m's more global effects: "A culture approaching pure S&M Gothic would be one where human relations, especially erotic relations, would always be defined as power relations. Equality in love, as well as politics and social life generally, would no longer be a tenable ideal. It would be impossible in such a culture to conceive of any relation, with husband, with child, with neighbor, or with friend, except in terms of domination and submission; in an S&M culture, love (if one could still use that word) would always be love of power."[46] You mean, if s/m stopped being theater for a minority and began being reality for everyone . . . ! That is the true problem with pure S&M Gothic. Read enough of it and you start to think in apocalyptic terms. And once you do, you are bound to want an effective alternative drive to avert the apocalypse.

Edmundson's own candidate is personified in Shelley's

Prometheus—a figure he favorably contrasts with the masochistic Freudian ego: "To Shelley, men and women ought to expect to do more than to live equably, ironically, and sanely, as Freud, in general, teaches we should. We are more than just egos bound to negotiate between the pleasure and reality principles until our races are run. At our best we are the ones who steal fire, the primal powers of nature, and with them create civilizations. . . . Prometheus is humankind as creator, not only in the arts, but also in the sciences."[47] What is wrong with this contrast—which pits the Gothic against the creative in a mythical battle of evil and good—is that it forgets that art and science are what give the reality principle much of its content, so that what living sanely requires is never settled or scripted, but always a matter for creativity, for art and science.

The Gothic—or Goth—in us is not something we can overcome once and for all. Power will always be erotically attractive. Edmundson sees that. What he fails to see is that when it takes the form of s/m, the Gothic is not something we should even want to overcome. The fire we steal from Jupiter can be so bright that the darkness of the dungeon, whatever its risks, may be exactly where our involvements occasionally need to go. There are far more dangerous places.

9

WORK AND/AS LOVE

Homer's Calypso is a nymph. She will always be beautiful. Her breasts will never sag. Her bottom will always be firm, her hair luxuriant and silky. She will always be fun in bed, and always, it seems, eager to go there. She is the closest thing to a Platonic Form, apparently, that a woman could be—a perfect satisfier of male sexual desire. Moreover, she can render her lover, too, Formlike—immortal and eternally young. No need for Rogaine, no need for Viagra. He will be vibrant and virile and hairy forever. Why would Odysseus— why would any man—leave all that for a mere mortal woman and his own incipient old age and death?

Penelope is probably around forty. Past childbearing, or soon to be past it, she isn't a babe. Yet more than a hundred princes (one hundred seventeen, by my count), young enough to be her sons, have been paying court to her for three years, camped out in her palace, eating and drinking, while she and they grow older. Of all the women in their world, she is the one they want for a wife—not just for an educational Mrs. Robinson–style roll in the hay, but for a wife.

When Achilles among the dead in Hades hears that his son has become a great warrior, he is temporarily reconciled even to the death he finds worse than being a slave—his steps are light as he leaves Odysseus (who has brought him the news), filled as he is "with joy at his son's preeminence."[1] By marrying Penelope, the suitors will almost certainly deprive themselves of such joy. What in a world like theirs, where sons are even more important than in ours, could possibly compensate them for that loss?

When Odysseus was the suitors' age, he wasn't sniffing around an older married woman with a bunch of other young men. He was getting ready to go to Troy, to win a reputation as a warrior that has become the stuff of song and story in his own lifetime—the Phaeacians are already singing of Troy when Odysseus washes up on their shores. We would never have heard of the suitors or Telemachus if Odysseus hadn't killed the former and fathered the latter. They aren't fit subjects for heroic poetry; he is. They can't so much as draw his bow. He can use it to shoot an arrow through a line of axe heads. He *is*. They are wannabes.

And what he is, first and foremost, is a great warrior, an immensely resourceful man—a survivor. Like Athena, his champion, he is intelligent, cunning, circumspect. What he likes to do is fight, compete in games that are like fighting and are training for it, feast with his friends, and hear the bards sing about great battles and great fighting men. He likes to tell the kinds of stories the *Odyssey* contains. This is who Odysseus is. Not to be that is for him a kind of social death almost as bad as the real thing.

When the Cyclops asks who is in his cave, Odysseus tricks him by answering, "Noman." But when he has blinded the Cyclops and escaped, he can't resist saying who he really is, so that this triumph too will redound to him:

> Cyclops, if anyone, any mortal man,
> Asks you how you got your eye put out,
> Tell him that Odysseus the marauder did it,
> Son of Laertes, whose home is on Ithaca![2]

The person Cyclops chooses to tell, however, is an *immortal*—his father, Poseidon, god of the sea. The storms that delay Odysseus' homecoming for ten years are the revenge he exacts for his son's blinding. At the cost of being Noman, Odysseus could have avoided the delaying storms, but that cost—even in the land of the Cyclopes—was too high.

The Cyclops episode is a particularly clear case. But everything else that happens to Odysseus, from the time he leaves Troy to the time he leaves Calypso, tells the same story. Circe, who turns men to swine, the Lotus-Eaters, who make men forget their homes and who they are, Hades, where the dead enjoy a semi-life—all are threats to Odysseus' identity. Calypso herself is just the first and most serious of them. Her island is so far off the beaten track that many of the things that make life worth living for Odysseus do not exist on it. There are no great feasts, no bards, and none of the wars and sports that give them something to sing about. Yet these, he tells the Phaeacians after he has left Calypso, are the best things life has to offer:

> Nothing we do is sweeter than this—
> A cheerful gathering of all the people
> Sitting side by side throughout the halls,
> Feasting and listening to a singer of tales,
> The table filled with food and drink,
> The server drawing wine from the bowl
> And bringing it around to fill our cups.
> For me this is the finest thing in the world.[3]

It is a passage Plato wants to excise from the text as harmful to potential soldiers or philosophers: eating and drinking are something they should want to do only to the extent necessary for good health.[4]

Calypso deprives Odysseus of the world that gives him meaning and provides the coordinates, so to speak, of his location in reality. Hence, the eternal life and youth she offers come at too high a price. To be Noman forever is no benefit. Sex *that* anonymous, even with a nymph, is not enough. Odysseus weeps on Ogygia and cannot wait to leave, because he wants to be again the Somebody that in the real world he is.

Something else is also missing on Ogygia. Calypso and Odysseus have been having sex nightly for seven years—that is about 2,500 times. Yet they have no children. And that absence signals another. On Ogygia, one day is like the next, the future like the past. In returning to Ithaca, therefore, where his only son lives, Odysseus is also returning to a place with a future, open and unscripted.

Ogygia is an unreal island—a fantasy place—as are all the others Odysseus visits on his way there. His travels are not through real space in the poem, because he isn't the real Odysseus while in them. So the apparently odd form of the poem—in which *Hamlet* (the drama of Penelope and the suitors) and *Sinbad the Sailor* (Odysseus' travels) seem incongruously intertwined—in fact reflects what the poem is about.

When Odysseus leaves Calypso and begins to travel toward the real Ithaca rather than away from it, his first port of call is Phaeacia, which is semi-real; Phaeacian ships are self-piloting, for example, but they travel to real places. There he meets his true self in the songs of the bard Demodocus, and begins to take on his own identity once more:

> I am Odysseus, great Laertes' son,
> Known for my cunning throughout the world
> And my fame reaches even to heaven.[5]

To heaven, yes. But also, of course, to the lands beneath it. And in that fact lies the answer to the mystery of the suitors and their desire for Penelope.

Just as men of my generation grew up in the 1950s hearing about the heroes of the Second World War, we know that Telemachus and the suitors grew up hearing about those of the Trojan war. On countless occasions they must have heard the bards sing of these great men. Their imaginations must have been filled with them and their exploits. How they must have wanted to be like them—to *be* them! This, I think, is the explanation the poem offers us of why the suitors are so young and why they want Penelope. They are young because they are the next generation—the ones who did not fight at Troy. They want Penelope because she is the wife of Odysseus. They want her because having her is like being Odysseus. Even being in her aura, just hanging around in Odysseus' palace, brings them closer to what they want than anything else.

There are two episodes which make us particularly aware of this. In the first, Athena comes to Ithaca in disguise to inspire Telemachus to find out about his father. She asks him if he is truly Odysseus' son. He replies:

> You want to know the truth, and I will give it to you.
> My mother says that Odysseus is my father.
> I don't know this myself.[6]

His uncertainty is rooted—where else?—in a doubt about worthiness: "Am I worthy to be Odysseus' son?" It is a question that must have found an analogue and a potential answer in the minds of each of the suitors: "*If* I can win Penelope, I am the equal of Odysseus; I am as good as the men of my father's generation; I am my father's son; I am a man."

In the second episode, Antinous, one of the most prominent of the suitors, describes the attraction Penelope holds for him:

> All the gifts Athena has given her,
> Her talent for handiwork, her good sense,
> Her cleverness—all of which go far beyond

That of any of the heroines of old,
Tyro or Alcmene or garlanded Mycene,
Not one of whom had a mind like Penelope's.[7]

These are odd traits to fire a young man's blood. Aphrodite's gifts should be more on his mind than Athena's. Antinous' description makes Penelope sound much like Odysseus. She is as good at women's work as he at men's —that's the only difference. What Antinous (as well as, by implication, the other suitors) admires in Penelope—what he wants in her—is her likeness to her husband. Odysseus is the real (though unconscious) object of his eros; she is (among other things, no doubt) its displaced object.

The women to whom Antinous compares Penelope seem selected simply to flatter. But there is more to it than that. All three had famous sons: Tyro was the mother of Peleus (the father of Achilles), Alcmene of Heracles, Mycene of Argos.[8] So in describing Penelope, a woman old enough to be his mother, Antinous not only imagines himself in Odysseus' place; he also imagines himself—Oedipally—in that of a famous son. Either the old block, he seems to say, or a chip off it.

The suitors are playing at being Odysseus. But they are doing so in a world where men like Odysseus really exist. Therein lies the danger of their fantasy. When Odysseus comes home and fully takes on his identity, the fantasy is over, and the awful reality—*his* awful reality—destroys them. It reveals them for what they really are: shadows only, not the thing itself. Their punishment, which seems so extreme, is nothing but the punishment reality imposes on fantasists. It is neither just nor unjust—it's simply what happens.

The identity of Odysseus is at the heart of the *Odyssey*. It is the sun around which all else in the poem revolves. But it is an identity that Homer reveals as being at odds with itself. Odysseus goes to Troy to punish Paris for stealing Helen. He goes to defend home and family. But to do so he must leave his own home and family undefended. Implicit in these facts is the deep Homeric thought of how ill-suited the hero himself is to his own home, and of how ill-suited home is, therefore, to serve as his life's goal. Odysseus' return shows this. He comes home not to be a peaceful head of household, but to be a warrior again, protecting his palace as once he destroyed Priam's—and for the same reason. When his work is done, he will have to leave again, traveling so far from the sea that his oar will be mistaken for a winnowing fan; so far that no one there will have heard of the Greek fleet that set sail for Troy, or even of the sea on which their ships were launched; so far that Odysseus himself will be Noman again. Then he can go home—to die.

The near paradox of desire the *Odyssey* leaves us with is part of its immense legacy to love. Love opens a space—Odysseus' palace in Ithaca—for intimacy. It places in it objects of desire: Penelope, the great rooted bed in which she and Odysseus sleep. Then, in order to protect that space from other desirers, love must develop capacities for violence that make their possessor unfit to live there. Odysseus can love Penelope only as someone to go back to for a short while. He can't live with her all the time. He would get bored and need to do something to prove to himself that he is who he is. The husband who builds a cozy house for his family and then has to leave it for the harsh, competitive world of work is Odysseus' heir and inherits many of his problems.

Vincent (Aurélien Recoing), the main character in Laurent Cantet's film *Time Out*, is one such heir.[9] He finds his job as a "consultant" so meaningless and depressing that he cracks. Instead of keeping his appointments, he drives around in his comfortable car, smoking, listening to music, thinking of nothing. Eventually, he gets fired. On the surface, the film seems to be about the ego-destroying effects of unemployment. And to some extent it is. But it is also about Vincent's conception of manhood and manly love and what it does to him.

Like his father, Vincent thinks a good father and husband is first and foremost a breadwinner, a good provider of material well-being and comfort. But what his father could readily and securely provide in his more predictable and traditional world, Vincent cannot: his father's house is solid, built to last; his own is see-through, insubstantial, gimcrack by comparison. When loss of his job threatens his role as provider, Vincent responds by trying to ensure that for his family, at least, nothing significant will change. He tells them he has quit in order to take a better—but fabricated—job with the UN, across the border in Geneva.

He raises money, first, by borrowing from his father for

a fictitious apartment, then by duping his friends with a get-rich-quick scheme, then by getting involved in smuggling fake consumer goods manufactured in eastern Europe. The spectral nature of much modern work (it is never clear what anyone actually *does*), the increasingly notional distinction between legitimate and black markets, between genuine articles and knock-offs, is one of the film's organizing themes.

When Vincent's family finds out about his deception, his eldest son is outraged: "You bullshitted us," he says. Black-market Reebok knock-offs are as good as the real thing—if the price is right. But when it comes to love, appearances aren't enough. He can *feel* the difference. His well-named younger brother, Félix, provides an even clearer illustration. Because he is still incompletely socialized, he treats cost as a function of value, not of market forces. When he is selling his toys at a school fair, he charges less for one toy than another comparable one not because it cost less, but because he likes it less. Similarly, when the beans are spilled, only Félix treats Vincent as he did before. Daddy, for him, is still just the one you feel a certain way toward, not the one who does what fathers are socially supposed to do. Vincent himself is finally led to abandon his deceit because of its effects on his wife, Muriel (Karin Viard), and its potential to harm a friend he cheats but feels enough for to repay.

The friend in question, whose family Vincent wistfully envies, is a hippy househusband who stays at home in his modest apartment making music and playing with his daughter, while his wife supports them all. The suggestion seems to be that untraditional, "feminized" men can escape Vincent's fate. Still, it isn't overplayed. This untraditional family, too, is part of Vincent's world. Eager—as everyone except the not yet socialized boy is—for easy money, they hand over their modest savings to Vincent in the hope of getting rich. "We were keeping it for bad times," they say, "but the bad times never seem to come." Vincent, for whom the bad times *have* come, knows better how vulnerable they really are.

In the penultimate scene, Vincent runs away from his life, driving into the night in his sheltering car. Then he pulls off the road, leaves the car, and seems to be walking to his death on the highway glimpsed ahead. In the final scene, after an abrupt cut, he is in a job interview arranged by his father. The equivalence of work and death is powerfully established. "I run on enthusiasm," he tells the interviewer. It is an emotion he has never exhibited.

Vincent's upbringing has shaped him to love by breadwinning. He can no more renegotiate that fact than he can fly. But what breadwinning requires of him leaves him empty—with little else to give in the way of love. He can't abandon Muriel and his kids. But staying with them means he must sacrifice his life for theirs. It is an Odyssean arrangement. Vincent, we feel, will soon be taking time out again.

Just as Oedipus, to his ruin, had one foot in traditional religion and one in the new world of secular knowledge, Vincent has one foot in the traditional world of his father, another in the untraditional one of his children. It is that uncomfortable position, the film suggests, that screws him. If Richard Sennett is right, he is not alone. In his book *The Corrosion of Character*, Sennett tells a similar story about a father and son, and about the impact of changes in their patterns of work on the intelligibility of their love stories. Enrico (the father) worked as a janitor, cleaning toilets and mopping floors in a downtown office building. He did so uncomplainingly, because "his work had one single and durable purpose, the service of his family."[10] After fifteen years, he had saved enough money to leave his old Italian neighborhood for a house in the suburbs. Then his wife got a job as a presser in a cleaning plant. By 1970, when Sennett first interviewed them, they were saving for the college education of their two sons.

"What had most struck me," he writes, "about Enrico and his generation was how linear time was in their lives: year after year of working in jobs that seldom varied from day to day. And along that line of time, achievement was cumulative." Moreover, the period in which they lived was predictable: "The upheavals of the Great Depression and World War II had faded, unions protected their jobs; though he was only forty when I first met him, Enrico knew precisely when he would retire and how much money he would have. . . . His life thus made sense to him as a linear narrative."[11]

The scaffolding of this narrative is political—peace and prosperity, the existence of unions with seniority rules, government pension schemes, and so on. It is also psychological. Enrico needs the self-discipline, the ability to postpone gratification and make sacrifices for his family, that amounts to having a character of a certain familiar type: loyal, industrious, steadfast, self-sacrificing. To live out the narrative, he needs to *be* that character.

Rico (the son) has fulfilled his father's dream. He has degrees in electrical engineering and business and runs his own consulting firm. His wife manages a big team of accountants. Their income, on the national scale, is in the top 5 percent. They are equal working partners, moving from place to place sometimes because of his work, sometimes because of hers. In fourteen years, they have moved four times. That is a lot of moves—and there may well be more ahead: "Today, a young American with at least two years of college can expect to change jobs eleven times in the course of working, and change his or her skill base at least three times during those forty years of labor." What this means, in effect, is that "the traditional career progressing step by step through the corridors of one or two institutions is withering." Linear narratives in which experience, advancement, and wealth are cumulative have ceased to apply. Jobs have been replaced with projects, hierarchies with networks. The fastest-growing sector of the American labor force consists of "people who work for temporary job agencies." The motto everywhere has become "No long term."[12] In a world in which "instability is meant to be normal" and "uncertainty exists . . . without any looming historical disaster," it is a motto of wisdom.[13] Acting as if there is a long term in such a world would simply make you incapable of the supple responsiveness to rapidly changing and uncertain circumstances that alone ensures profitability and survival. But that world, in turn, is largely a product of a market that is "'consumer-driven' as never before in history"—a market in which the "desire for rapid return" has caused the average time stocks are held to drop 60 percent in the past fifteen years.[14]

The short-term behavior and "chameleon values" that promote success in the modern workplace seem in tension, however, with the long-term virtues, such as "formal obligations, trustworthiness, commitment, and purpose," that Sennett—and even Rico—think are required in the intimate sphere. Since a worthwhile life involves both work and intimacy, they are therefore forced to confront hard questions: "How can long-term purposes be pursued in a short-term society? How can durable social relations be sustained? How can a human being develop a narrative of identity and life history in a society composed of episodes and fragments?"[15] Sennett's answer, given on the book's final page, is that "a regime which provides human beings no deep reasons to care about one another cannot long preserve its legitimacy."[16] This seems true enough. What is controversial is the implication that selves forged in Sennett's modern workplace will have no such reasons. But if they won't, and if caring about one another is a condition of love, the future of love looks pretty bleak.

That is only part of Sennett's story, however—the part that applies to ordinary working stiffs. A different part altogether applies to the bosses, the movers and shakers. "The capacity to let go of one's past, the confidence to accept fragmentation: these are two traits of character which appear . . . among people truly at home in the new capitalism." And they are no mere isolated traits. Like trustworthiness, commitment, and the rest, they constitute a particular type of character—"that of someone who has the confidence to dwell in disorder, someone who flourishes in the midst of dislocation."[17] With such a character, you could be among the Bill Gateses of the world, one of the "rulers of the flexible realm," the "new masters," who have "rejected careers in the old English sense of the word, as pathways along which people can travel." But if you "work lower down in the flexible regime," if you are an ordinary person, "the same traits of character begetting spontaneity become more self-destructive," since they cannot give "any guidance for the conduct of an ordinary life."[18]

It is an oddly schizophrenic picture and, again, an Odyssean one: the new masters of the flexible regime are as unfit for intimate life, apparently, as the old warrior. Yet the assumption that viable love stories have to be traditional ones like Enrico's seems problematic. Why can't improvisation be a genre of romance? Why can't the supple adaptivity required for success on the job be the basis of a new style of intimate life in which ordinary people develop the traits now reserved for the new masters? This style may not be the traditional family style. But so what? Maybe the suppleness children acquire by moving from one place to another as their parents change jobs, from one parent to another as spouses divorce, or from one sort of Lebensraum to another as people change sexual preferences or income groups, is just what they will need when they finally leave home for the world their parents have bequeathed them.

"If we think of the world's future," Ludwig Wittgenstein writes, "we always mean the place it will get to if it keeps going as we see it going now, and it doesn't occur to us that it is not going in a straight line but in a curve and that its direction is constantly changing."[19] Love and families, too, are going in a curve—one we are in no position to plot or much control. This causes anxiety, especially in parents. So there is a tendency—exhibited by Sennett and Rico—to try to quiet it by resorting to what Svetlana Boym calls "restorative nostalgia": we try to return family traditions to the way (we think) they used to be in the good old days—and keep them like that.[20]

The problem is that these traditions led to the supposedly decadent ones we have now. Nostalgically restored, they lead only to the place V. S. Naipaul presciently predicted for Mobutu's Zaïre more than twenty years ago: "Mobutu's . . . kingship is sterile. The cult of the king already swamps the intellectual advance of a people who have barely emerged. The intellectual confusions of authenticity that now give such an illusion of power, close up the world again and point to a future greater despair."[21] The present illusion of power, the closed-up world, the future greater despair are the costs of trying to remove love and families from Wittgenstein's curve, of trying to embalm or Platonize them.

In the rest of the animal kingdom, sex and reproduction are closely linked—so closely that we can speak of the sexual instinct as the reproductive one. The invention of effective contraceptives, especially the birth-control pill, brought about a revolution in our love lives by separating the two. One result, is that sex has become something we can have—and maybe even admit to wanting—just for itself, without love or marriage. Another is that we no longer need to take at face value the phenomenon of love at first sight. It may just be lust or romantic infatuation—something that doesn't have to lead to Lebensraum construction to achieve its goals.

Once love gets distinguished from lust and romantic infatuation in this way, it tends to be seen in a different and more practical light. It requires getting to know another person, testing for compatibility, thinking about shared interests, the economic viability of the partnership, and the equitable sharing of household chores. As romance becomes pleasure, love becomes more like work ("We have to work on our relationship"). But love is not all work. It is also—crucially—passion and romance. Having taken the romance out of it, so to speak, we are faced with having to put it back in somehow.

A popular model of how to do this is punctuated equilibrium—with love providing the equilibrium, romance the punctuation. You can gauge its popularity from the fact that whole industries exist to help script the punctuations, the "romantic interludes." An intimate dinner with a good bottle of wine? The restaurant industry is there to sell it to us. A getaway for two to a South Sea island beach? The tourist industry. Interflora, Hallmark, Victoria's Secret . . . All you need is a credit card. Of course, it isn't as if you just had these ideas about what romance consists in and then the market obligingly responded. It is rather that the market, through advertising, movies, television, magazines, and other mass media, sold you both the ideas and the (consuming) ways to put them into practice. Romance, like fashion, is off the rack. It is work's way of helping love and romance—and work itself, of course—to peacefully coexist.

The humdrum punctuated by the generic may not sound all that alluring. Yet the alternation of the two, according to Eva Illouz, somehow manages to breathe life into both at once: "Contrary to popular laments that marriage is threatened by the fading of the emotional intensity of the 'beginnings,' my analysis suggests that the everyday—monotonous, wearing, pedestrian—is the symbolic pole from which moments of romantic exaltation draw their meaning. Such moments are significant precisely because they are short-lived and unsustainable in daily life. Far from marking a 'dwindling' of love, the entry into the 'profane' realm of daily life (usually the realm of marriage) begins a rhythmic alternation with 'sacred' romantic modes of interaction. The stability of married life depends on sustaining this rhythm."[22] Get in the right groove, Illouz suggests, and love, work, and romance will all fit tidily together.

Well, they will fit tidily together for some, but not for others. The "educated post-modern lover," aware of "the ubiquitous use of romance to sell commodities," sees that "in the privacy of our words and acts of love, we rehearse cultural scenarios that we did not write." So she "treats her romantic beliefs with the skeptical irony of a post-Marxian and post-Freudian consciousness." The "culturally deprived," on the other hand, still continue to find the "formulas of romance" compelling. The cost of cultural wealth is "cultural alienation"; the cost of cultural deprivation is inauthenticity—and, of course, a mounting credit-card bill.[23]

Just as an autobiography subjects a particular life to the ordeal of "exposure to the light of day," so a cultural scenario, as a type of ritual, does the same to a particular form of life. And just as there is no guarantee that the particular life will stand up to the test, there is no guarantee that the form of life will either. The possibility of a failed autobiography—of an autobiography that represents an achievement not in self-knowledge but in self-ignorance or self-concealment or self-falsification—reveals as much. Even if the formulas of romance I employ are my very own, their picture of love might not survive exposure. It might repel "calm and steady contemplation . . . on the part of someone who offers it full and informed attention."[24] On the other hand, merely having been used to sell commodities doesn't ensure that the formulas of romance will fail this test. Great art is used to sell commodities, and has even become a commodity itself, without losing one whit of its capacity to pass it.

"A book is a mirror," the aphorist Georg Christoph Lichtenberg wrote. "If an ape looks into it, an apostle is hardly likely to look out."[25] A cultural scenario is similar: what we bring to it partly determines what we find there. We didn't invent the forms of torture favored in our culture, for example, and our reaction to them is scarcely original: we scream. Yet no amount of irony—no amount of cultural capital—will alienate us from them. Physical pain, as Wilde puts it, "wears no mask," and so is immune to being seen through.[26] As a result, torture is a mirror that reveals the suffering animal in all who look into it. Our formulas of romance are certainly more susceptible to ironic unmasking. But since they have infantile roots, they tend to retain some of their power to pain or please even in the face of it. So against them, too, irony's aggressive defenses are less than perfectly effective.

Ilouz's use of the terms "sacred" and "profane" implicitly analogizes romance to morning and evening prayers, which punctuate for the faithful the profane day of work and home life. It is an analogy hospitable to the market, since it portrays romance as a discrete area of experience with its own special commodities and modes of consumption. The resulting commercialization, which threatens romance while apparently facilitating it, has a similar effect on spirituality. We want to have a personal relationship with God. But what we say to him is what everyone else says. In Christian supply stores, you can buy prayers composed by jingle writers.

Prayer can also be thought of in another way, however: not as something that takes place only at night or in the morning, but something we can turn our entire day into by offering it to God, by living it in the right spirit. Part of that spirit consists in not forgetting God's presence in the space our love has opened also for other things— friends, family, play, learning. Instead of punctuated equilibrium, in which the tedium of the everyday is relieved by moments of romantic fantasy, the tedium is now transformed by its goal. Work done for love—even if that work is fighting a war—is different from work done for other reasons. The romance can be chivalric, as it were. It can consist not simply in providing a paycheck, but in providing, as in Vincent's case, a love gift—a gift of the (working) self. Just how costly a gift it may prove to be is another matter.

IO

SEX, DEMOCRACY, AND THE FUTURE OF LOVE

During the 1970s, historian Gérard Vincent tells us, "sexual harmony became the structural principle of the couple." Duty, reciprocal devotion, children were no longer essential. Values had shifted "toward greater emphasis on individual and/or conjugal narcissism," precipitating or constituting "the major event affecting private life in Western societies in recent decades." As a result, the couple allegedly became "a three-way affair, involving a man, a woman, and a third party (confessor, psychoanalyst, sexologist)."[1] Allegedly, too, the "novel of love"—the genre par excellence of intimate life—was "superseded by the novel that explores the primacy of our sexual selves."[2] "Almost the first question I ask about a character that I'm about to get going," says novelist Martin Amis, "is 'What are they like in the sack?'"[3]

Whereas Vincent focuses on sexual harmony, others

tell us that a "particular form of intimacy, 'disclosing intimacy'—a process of two or more people mutually sustaining deep knowing and understanding, through talking and listening, sharing thoughts, showing feelings—is increasingly sought in personal life."[4] Since disclosing intimacy doesn't seem to mandate any particular kind of sexuality, the two may seem to have little to do with each other. Not so, sociologist Anthony Giddens argues. In a relationship of disclosing intimacy, sexuality must be "plastic." It must be freed from the "needs of reproduction" and "the rule of the phallus," so as to become "a life-style issue" rather than a fate.[5] In the pre-Freudian (and now, I think, outmoded) sense, it must be perverse: "The macho gay, the leather queen, the denim groupie . . . are a visible deconstruction of maleness, and at the same time they affirm what taken for granted phallic power denies: that, in modern social life, self-identity, including sexual identity, is a reflexive achievement."[6] Rather than violating the laws of nature, "perverts" show us that what we took to be natural laws are in fact choices, aspects of freedom, that reveal "the general importance of homosexual desire, even for those who don't act on it."[7]

The Giddens-style love story, whose heroes are appropriately self-disclosing and sexually plastic, is "Intimacy as Democracy." In outline, at least, its plot is straightforward and familiar—in one form or another—from popular psychology. Intimate disclosure requires firm personal boundaries: soft ones lead to autonomy-threatening codependency. It requires freedom from violence and coercion, as well as mutual respect; without them disclosure is bound to be inhibited or distorted. Openness is also essential, since "an individual whose real intentions are hidden from a partner" prevents her from autonomously "determining the conditions of their association." None of these prerequisites can exist, however, without a balance of power, "the increasing autonomy of women," and a "plastic sexuality, no longer harnessed to the double standard."[8]

Yet since plasticity is designed to allow individuals to become, sexually speaking, who they are, it mustn't require them to be risqué, if what turns them on is to be middle-of-the-road. A sexuality that involves being willing—as Foucault claims s/m adepts are—to invent new possibilities of pleasure with strange parts of their body may be just the ticket for some people, but others may prefer something a lot closer to tradition. What Montreal psychotherapist Alison Carpenter refers to as PIVMO—penile intromission in the vagina with male orgasm—may not be for us, but if nothing gives John and Mary greater pleasure (not even mutual orgasm), who are we to force them to change their ways? Pleasure, given its biological and infantile origins, is not guaranteed to be on the side of transparency, nonviolence, and respect—which means that the gender roles we reject at one level may reappear through the very door intimacy-as-democracy requires us to keep open.

Giddens himself, while he recognizes the possibility of such a reappearance, is cautiously optimistic about it: "In lesbian relationships (as among male gays also), attitudes and traits 'prohibited' in the pure relationship can potentially be acted upon, including instrumental control and the exercise of formal power. Confined within the sphere of sexuality and turned into fantasy—rather than, as has always been usual, determined from the outside—dominance perhaps helps to neutralize aggression which would otherwise make itself felt elsewhere."[9] Since the sphere of (post-Freudian) sexuality isn't the bedroom or any other readily isolatable area, the caution is surely warranted. The idea that there is a clear outside to it, therefore, where all real dominance resides, while that sphere itself remains intrinsically pure, potentially democratic, and tolerant only of fantasy dominance, is a lot more comforting than credible.

For the disclosing couple, eroticism is supposedly an "art of giving and receiving pleasure" that "grows out of friendship and caring," rather than out of "passion confused with fear."[10] Given sexual pleasure's deep roots, this may help explain why such a couple will tend to become a three-way affair of the sort Vincent describes: analysts, therapists, and sexologists are needed to help them uncover the pleasures it is their raison d'être to give and receive. "What are couples for," Adam Phillips asks, "if they are not for pleasure?"[11] Once experts are invited into the intimate sphere, however, it changes from a private sphere into a semi-public one subject to moral and political norms. As a result, the pleasures we give and receive within it tend to become normalized. What is plastic, notoriously, is easily molded.

Georges Bataille, troubled by the growing popularity of so-called sexual liberation, once remarked to Octavio Paz:

"Eroticism is inseparable from violence and transgression. Eroticism is an infraction, and if prohibitions disappeared, it too would disappear. And with it, mankind, at least as we have known it since the Paleolithic."[12] We don't have to go all the way with Bataille to recognize how pallid Giddens' normalized eroticism threatens to become.

The metaphor of disclosure represents the self as an entity needing primarily to be known and understood, and so as realizing itself most fully in intimate communication. The larger world where money is earned, wars fought, societies politically transformed, art produced, and scientific discoveries made is as alien to that self, apparently, as to the archetypal suburban house. Denuded of everything except its own intimate thoughts and feelings, it must nonetheless provide at least half the resources needed to sustain a relationship. Since it is the rare self that can manage such a task, one hardly needs vast empirical research to be persuaded that "few people sustain relationships, even friendships, which are based exclusively on disclosing intimacy separated from mutually negotiated practical assistance."[13]

Intimacy often does involve the revealing of intimate information, to be sure, and the meshing of souls available only within shared daily life. But it also typically involves shared interests distinct from the partners' interest in each other. When we talk about a movie we have both seen, or a book we have both read, or a person we both know, we learn about each other, but also about books, movies, and people. We interest our lovers, as we interest other people, by being interesting about interesting things. Maybe love used to be "woman's whole existence."[14] Nowadays, it isn't anyone's (at least, ideally). Were it everyone's, boredom would lay waste our lives.

What our lover sees about us isn't what no one else sees, but a larger whole that includes it. The intimate self is not a special entity with special needs and a special form of life; it is the familiar person with some of his needs particularly highlighted. Among these, we may allow, is a need to communicate intimacies, the heart's secrets. But deep as that need may be, the need not to communicate them—indeed, not to communicate at all—may be equally deep. Self-disclosing is an exhausting and anxiety-inducing business. From it—as from reason, self-control, and most other things in life—our involvements occasionally need to shift. So within a tolerable and sustainable intimacy, there must be places for it to shift to—sanctuaries from disclosure that intimacy itself creates.

Typically, sex is accessible from within intimacy. (Many think, indeed, that it should be accessible only from there —or, which is not at all the same thing, from within monogamous heterosexual marriage.) Nonetheless, sex isn't itself an intrinsically intimate place—if by that we mean a place where intimate self-disclosure is bound to occur. Anonymous sex isn't a contradiction in terms; neither is commercial sex. A man putting his cock through a hole in a toilet wall for another to suck isn't disclosing much of himself. Sometimes, even when we are in an intimate loving relationship, that is the sort of sex we want. We want to be an anonymous cock (mouth, anus . . .) for a lover who is being an anonymous cunt (mouth, anus . . .) for us. Though few of us want to be just a sex object, most of us want a lover who wants to be, and wants us to be, a sex object occasionally. It is only when we take our moral and political identities too inflexibly to bed that such desires become too awful to admit to or satisfy.

Leo Bersani thinks that all sex is intrinsically impersonal, because it is person-shattering. "We desire what nearly shatters us," he writes, "and the shattering experience is, it would seem, *without any specific content*—which may be our only way of saying that the experience cannot be said, that it belongs to the nonlinguistic biology of human life."[15] That is why Candace Vogler can characterize him as "a delicious antidote to the widespread impulse to harness sexuality firmly to carts carrying happy selves towards egalitarian camaraderie."[16]

More recently, a very different sort of writer and thinker, Simon Blackburn, has mobilized the same insight in a somewhat different way. Orgasm *is* depersonalizing, he thinks. Yet it is not objectifying in the morally repugnant sense: "At the time of crisis, it is probably true that lovers are not treating their partners decorously or with respect or as fully self-directed moral agents. But that is because strictly speaking they are not treating them any way at all, either as persons or as objects. In the frenzy they are lost to the world, way beyond that. . . . The body has taken over, saturated with excitement and desire. But this is marvelous, even if moments of rapture mean a pause in the conversation."[17] There is truth, I think, and not just antidotal truth, in Bersani's and

Blackburn's remarks. All the same, what shatters me may not be what shatters you; what causes your crisis may leave me cold. When we make each other come, both of us may be shattered, unable to send or receive messages. Or what we send and receive may be beyond words. Yet because it is *you* making me come in the way only you know how to do, and vice versa, something is communicated. There is sex and sex. Some of it is very personal, some very impersonal, and it can be an important part of intimacy either way.

"Once upon a time," journalist Tracey Cox writes, "we committed for life. This morphed into serial monogamy—a series of long-term committed relationships that lasted years, but not a lifetime. The trend now is for need-based relationships: relationships that suit our circumstances at the time and finish when the situation changes."[18] It sounds—and is intended to sound—stylishly hard-nosed. Yet Cox simply assumes that our circumstance-suited needs will still constitute a unified—though perhaps short-lived—self which one other such self can best satisfy. But why accept her assumption? Why not think, instead, that needs will divide the class of partners more finely: X for sex; Y for children; Z for living with? Why not think that the couple—even the short-lived, need-related one—will morph into an n-tuple? No doubt, n cannot become all that large. Who could handle the complexity? But there is no obvious reason to think it would inevitably be two.

Among our deepest needs, "as urgent as are our physiological needs for food, drink, and sex," is our need to relieve boredom "with stimulating physical or mental activities."[19] So need-based love—indeed love of any sort—has to take boredom seriously. When people died at thirty, had little leisure, and no reliable birth control, that may not have been a particularly onerous erotic task: life was short and busy and child-filled enough for boredom not to be much of a problem. An erotic norm of life-long monogamous love was compatible with satisfying physiological needs for stimulation. We live too long now and have too many holidays and are used to too much excitement for that to be simply taken for granted.

The threat boredom poses is particularly acute if, as Gérard Vincent claims, sexual harmony has indeed become the couple's structural principle. Custom, after all, has a tendency to stale even near-infinite sexual variety in a partner. Eventually, what we come to want is a new partner, not something new with an old one. Why not decouple sex from coupling, then, and encourage partners either to find another structural principle for their relationship or another, less exclusively bivalent organization of the old one? It is a good question, but one that political reality threatens to render moot.

In the United States and other Western countries, most people agree that sex should be taught in schools. They disagree, however, about what form such education should take. Traditionalists (often but not always basing their views in religious teachings) believe that "the sole permitted, and morally esteemed, form of sexual activity is heterosexual coitus between a married couple." Liberals (often but not always secular in their moral views) believe that "whatever is freely and knowingly consented to by competent adults and doesn't harm third parties is morally permissible." Since sexual values are likely to be somewhat determinative of lifestyle more generally, a child whose sexual values his parents think mistaken is likely to have a life they regard as "blighted and unworthy." Thus, in a liberal democratic society which strives for neutrality between competing conceptions of the good life, sex education in public schools is bound to send deeply conflicted messages.[20]

Even if the messages were less conflicted, however, they—like Giddens' intimate democracy—would run up against something sex education alone cannot change. "In the beginning," as Adam Phillips puts it, "every child is an only child. . . . Our first inklings, that is to say, are monogamous ones: of privilege and privacy, of ownership and belonging. The stuff of which monogamy will be made."[21] To the extent that our first inklings remain monogamous, therefore, any attempt to change the norms of conventional love risks severing the heart from all its natural origins.

Still, this is a chicken-and-egg issue. *Our* first inklings of love were monogamous, private, and possessive. But when Mommy and Daddy have full-time jobs, neither has more than a part of him- or herself to give, even to a child. Other caregivers, including Daddy, have to help Mommy out. And that means the familiar infantile *pas de deux* will change. We may have drunk in monogamous, heterosexual, racially homogenous love with our mother's milk, but our children and our children's children probably won't. They may have two fathers, or two mothers, or a gay biological father, a straight white birth mother, and a Eurasian bisexual primary caregiver. Monogamy for them, like sexual identity for Giddens' democratic intimates, may turn out to be a lifestyle issue, a reflexive achievement.

"The mystery of what a couple is, exactly," novelist Mavis Gallant assures us, "is almost the only true mystery left to us, and when we have come to the end of it there will be no more need for literature—or for love for that matter."[22] Will we have come to that end when coupling ceases to be a fate? I doubt it. But even if we have, the more general mystery of the n-tuple will be there to take its place. For even if it isn't monogamous coupling that we drink in with our mother's milk, it is likely to be something equally mysterious, equally inspiring of literature, equally problematic for our love lives.

NOTES

1. AGAPE, EROS, AND THE WILL

1. Matthew 22:37-39. *The New English Bible with Apocrypha* (New York: Oxford University Press, Cambridge University Press, 1970).
2. Harry G. Frankfurt, *Necessity, Volition, and Love* (Cambridge: Cambridge University Press, 1999), p. 133.
3. Benjamin Constant, *Adolphe,* trans. Leonard Tancock (Harmondsworth: Penguin Books, 1964), p. 73.
4. William Shakespeare, *King Lear,* I.i.101-106.
5. "Agapêseis ton plêsion sou hôs seauton."
6. Søren Kierkegaard, *Works of Love,* trans. David Swenson (Princeton: Princeton University Press, 1949), p. 47.
7. Ibid., p. 48.
8. Ibid., p. 37.
9. Ibid.
10. Ibid., p. 48.
11. Immanuel Kant, *Lectures on Ethics,* ed. Peter Heath and J. B. Schneewind, trans. Peter Heath (Cambridge: Cambridge University Press, 1997), p. 155.

12. Ibid., pp. 158–159.

13. Manfred Kuehn, *Kant: A Biography* (Cambridge: Cambridge University Press, 2001), p. 116.

14. Vladimir Nabokov, *Pnin* (Harmondsworth: Penguin Books, 1960), p. 17.

15. Friedrich Nietzsche, *Beyond Good and Evil,* trans. Walter Kaufmann (New York: Vintage Books, 1966), p. 81.

16. Junichirô Tanizaki, *Naomi,* trans. Anthony H. Chambers (London: Pan Books, 1987), p. 131.

17. Ibid., p. 129.

18. Ibid., p. 186.

19. Philip Fisher, *The Vehement Passions* (Princeton: Princeton University Press, 2002), pp. 98–99.

20. Octavio Paz, *The Double Flame: Love and Eroticism,* trans. Helen Lane (New York: Harcourt Brace, 1995), pp. 125, 40.

21. La Bruyère, "Du Coeur," no. 11, *Les Caractères.* My translation.

22. E. M. Forster, *The Longest Journey* (Harmondsworth: Penguin Books, 2001), pp. 330–331.

23. Albert Camus, *The First Man,* trans. David Hapgood (New York: Knopf, 1995), p. 311.

24. Michel de Montaigne, "On Friendship," *The Complete Essays,* trans. M. A. Screech (Harmondsworth: Penguin Books, 1991), p. 212.

25. Anders Nygren, *Eros and Agape* (Chicago: University of Chicago Press, 1982), p. 78.

26. Paz, *The Double Flame,* pp. 153–154.

2. SEEING, IMPROVISING, AND SELF-LOVE

1. Immanuel Kant, *Practical Philosophy,* ed. and trans. Mary J. Gregor (Cambridge: Cambridge University Press, 1996), p. 55.

2. Iris Murdoch, *Existentialists and Mystics,* ed. Peter Conradi (Harmondsworth: Penguin Books, 1998), pp. 219–220.

3. Ibid., p. 215.

4. Ibid., pp. 368–369.

5. Ibid., p. 354.

6. Ibid., p. 331.

7. Ibid., p. 215.

8. Ibid., p. 371.

9. Ibid., p. 375.

10. Ibid., p. 378.

11. Richard Wollheim, *On the Emotions* (New Haven: Yale University Press, 1999), p. 15.

12. Murdoch, *Existentialists and Mystics,* p. 321.

13. Ibid., p. 384.

14. Ibid., pp. 317–318.

15. Ibid., p. 354.

16. Ibid., p. 361.

17. J. M. Coetzee, *Youth* (London: Secker and Warburg, 2002), p. 3.

18. Philip Larkin, "Marriages," in Larkin, *Collected Poems,* ed. Anthony Thwaite (New York: Farrar Straus Giroux, 1989), p. 63.

19. Charles Baxter, *Saul and Patsy* (New York: Pantheon, 2003), p. 300.

20. E. M. Forster, *Howards End* (Harmondsworth: Penguin Books, 2000), p. 205.

21. Marcel Proust, *The Fugitive,* in *Remembrance of Things Past,* trans. C. K. Scott-Moncrieff, Terence Kilmartin, and Andreas Mayor (New York: Random House, 1981), vol. 3, p. 627.

22. Philip Roth, *American Pastoral* (New York: Houghton Mifflin, 1997), p. 35.

23. Friedrich Nietzsche, *Gesammelte Werke* (Munich: Musarion Verlag, 1920–1929), vol. 3, p. 245 (notebook from the period of *The Birth of Tragedy*). Quoted in Werner J. Dannhauser, *Nietz-*

sche's View of Socrates (Ithaca: Cornell University Press, 1974), p. 121, note 127.

24. I Corinthians 13:12, *The New English Bible with Apocrypha* (New York: Oxford University Press, Cambridge University Press, 1970).

25. J. David Velleman, "Love as a Moral Emotion," *Ethics,* 109 (1999), p. 361.

26. "If I love you, what business is it of yours?" J. W. von Goethe, *Wilhelm Meister's Apprenticeship,* Book 4, Chapter 9.

27. Anita Brookner, *The Bay of Angels* (New York: Random House, 2001), p. 166.

28. Philip Roth, *The Counterlife* (New York: Farrar Straus Giroux, 1986), pp. 320–321.

29. William Gibson, *Pattern Recognition* (New York: Putnam, 2003), p. 69.

30. Leda Cosmides and John Tooby, "Cognitive Adaptations for Social Exchange," in Jerome H. Barkow, Leda Cosmides, and John Tooby, eds., *The Adaptive Mind: Evolutionary Psychology and the Generation of Culture* (New York: Oxford University Press, 1992).

31. Cornelius Castoriadis, *World in Fragments,* ed. and trans. David Ames Curtis (Stanford: Stanford University Press, 1997), p. 155.

32. E. M. Forster, *A Passage to India* (Harmondsworth: Penguin Books, 2000), p. 197.

33. François Mauriac, *The Knot of Vipers,* trans. Gerard Hopkins (Harmondsworth: Penguin Books, 1985), p. 20.

34. Ibid., p. 52.

35. Ibid., p. 177.

36. Ibid., p. 182.

37. William Ian Miller, *Faking It* (Cambridge: Cambridge University Press, 2003), p. 153.

38. Sigmund Freud, *Civilization and Its Discontents,* in *The Standard Edition of the Complete Psychological Works of Sigmund Freud,* ed. and trans. James E. Strachey (London: Hogarth Press, 1995), vol. 21, p. 66.

39. Mykel Johnson, "Butchy Femme," in Joan Nestle ed., *The Persistent Desire: A Femme-Butch Reader* (Boston: Alyson Press, 1992), p. 396.

40. Quoted in Aileen M. Kelley, *Views from the Other Shore: Essays on Herzen, Chekhov, and Bakhtin* (New Haven: Yale University Press, 1999), p. 80. The excerpt is from Herzen, *Sobranie sochinenii* [Collected Works] (Moscow, 1954–1966), vol. 19, p. 184.

3. FIRST LOVE AND AFTER

1. Saint Augustine, *The City of God,* trans. R. W. Dyson (Cambridge: Cambridge University Press, 1998), p. 614.

2. Homer, *Iliad,* trans. Stanley Lombardo (Indianapolis: Hackett, 1997), p. 52 (Book 3, lines 53–66, of the Greek text).

3. James Joyce, *Ulysses* (New York: Random House, 1934), p. 173.

4. Lauren Berlant and Michael Warner, "Sex in Public," in Lauren Berlant, ed., *Intimacy* (Chicago: University of Chicago Press, 2000), p. 329.

5. Anthony Giddens, *The Transformation of Intimacy: Sexuality, Love, and Eroticism in Modern Societies* (Stanford: Stanford University Press, 1992), p. 31.

6. Adam Phillips, *On Kissing, Tickling, and Being Bored: Psychoanalytic Essays on the Unexamined Life* (Cambridge, Mass.: Harvard University Press, 1993), p. 4.

7. See Jacques Lacan, *Écrits: A Selection,* trans. Alan Sheridan (New York: Norton, 1977), pp. 1–7.

8. See Melanie Klein, *The Writings of Melanie Klein* (New York: Free Press, 1984), vol. 3, pp. 1–24.

9. Sigmund Freud, *The Ego and the Id,* in *The Standard Edition of the Complete Psychological Works of Sigmund Freud,* ed. and trans. James E. Strachey (London: Hogarth Press, 1995), vol. 19, p. 26.

10. D. W. Winnicott, *Playing and Reality* (Harmondsworth: Penguin Books, 1974), p. 130.

11. Sigmund Freud, *Three Essays on the Theory of Sexuality,* in *Standard Edition,* vol. 7, p. 222.

12. Giddens, *The Transformation of Intimacy,* p. 116.

13. Freud, *Three Essays,* p. 191.

14. Sigmund Freud, quoted in Ernest Jones, Th*e Life and Work of Sigmund Freud* (New York: Basic Books, 1955), vol. 2, p. 421.

15. K. Rotkin, "The Phallacy of our Sexual Norm," in A. G. Kaplan and J. P. Bean, eds., *Beyond Sex Role Stereotypes: Readings towards a Philosophy of Androgyny* (Boston: Little, Brown, 1976).

16. Jonathan Lear, *Love and Its Place in Nature* (New York: Farrar Straus Giroux, 1990), p. 153.

17. Pablo Neruda, *Memoirs,* trans. Hardie St. Martin (Harmondsworth: Penguin Books, 1978), p. 3.

18. Friedrich Nietzsche, *Untimely Meditations,* trans. R. J. Hollingdale (Cambridge: Cambridge University Press, 1983), p. 213.

19. Samuel Johnson, *The Rambler,* August 7, 1750.

20. Philip Larkin, "The Old Fools," in Larkin, *Collected Poems,* ed. Anthony Thwaite (New York: Farrar Straus Giroux, 1989), pp. 196–197.

21. Iris Murdoch, *The Black Prince* (London: Chatto and Windus, 1973), p. 9.

22. Marcel Proust, "The Fugitive," in *Remembrance of Things Past,* trans. C. K. Scott Moncrieff, Terence Kilmartin, and Andreas Mayor (New York: Random House, 1981), vol. 3, p. 541.

23. Friedrich Nietzsche, *The Will to Power,* trans. Walter Kaufmann (New York: Random House, 1967), p. 267.

4. ANXIETY AND THE ETHICS OF INTIMACY

1. Sigmund Freud, *Thoughts for the Times on War and Death,* in *The Standard Edition of the Complete Psychological Works of Sigmund Freud,* ed. and trans. James E. Strachey (London: Hogarth Press, 1995), vol. 14, p. 286.

2. W. B. Yeats, "Among School Children," in *The Collected Poems of W. B. Yeats* (New York: Macmillan, 1950), p. 214.

3. William Ian Miller, *The Anatomy of Disgust* (Cambridge, Mass.: Harvard University Press, 1997), p. xi.

4. Ibid., p. 101.

5. Immanuel Kant, *Lectures on Ethics,* ed. Peter Heath and J. B. Schneewind, trans. Peter Heath (Cambridge: Cambridge University Press, 1997), pp. 187–189.

6. Ibid., p. 201.

7. Norman Rush, *Mortals* (New York: Knopf, 2003), pp. 203–212.

8. E. M. Forster, *Howards End* (Harmondsworth: Penguin Books, 2000), p. 142.

9. Ibid., p. 205.

10. Ibid., pp. 207–210.

11. Ibid., pp. 262–263.

12. Ibid., p. 285.

13. Ibid., p. 220.

14. Ibid., pp. 207, 289–290.

15. Ibid., p. 290.

16. Ayn Rand, *Atlas Shrugged* (New York: Signet Books, 1996), p. 681.

17. Neera Badhwar, "Love," in Hugh LaFollette, ed., *The Oxford Handbook of Practical Ethics* (New York: Oxford University Press, 2002).

18. Anthony Trollope, *The Way We Live Now* (Oxford: Oxford University Press, 1982), p. 150.

19. Samuel Beckett, *Poems in English* (London: Calder and Boyers, 1961), p. 53.

20. See Philippa Foot, *Virtues and Vices* (Berkeley: University of California Press, 1978), pp. 1–18.

21. David Shapiro, *Neurotic Styles* (New York: Basic Books, 1965).

22. Thomas Mann, *The Magic Mountain* (New York: Knopf, 1927), p. 41.

23. Donald Meltzer, "Aesthetic Conflict: Its Place in the Developmental Process," in Meltzer, *The Apprehension of Beauty* (Perthshire: Clunie Press, 1988), p. 16.

5. JEALOUSY, PERVERSITY, AND OTHER LIABILITIES OF LOVE

1. Jean-Paul Sartre, *Being and Nothingness,* trans. Hazel E. Barnes (New York: Washington Square Press, 1971), pp. 478–479.

2. Marcel Proust, *The Captive,* in *Remembrance of Things Past,* trans. C. K. Scott Moncrieff, Terence Kilmartin, and Andreas Mayor (New York: Random House, 1981), vol. 3, pp. 98–105.

3. Adam Phillips, *On Flirtation* (Cambridge, Mass.: Harvard University Press, 1994), pp. xvii–xviii.

4. Eavan Boland, "Against Love Poetry," in Boland, *Against Love Poetry* (New York: Norton, 2001), p. 16.

5. George Crabb, *English Synonyms* (London: Routledge and Kegan Paul, 1974), p. 464.

6. John Berger, "Ernst Fischer: A Philosopher and Death," in Geoff Dyer, ed., *John Berger: Selected Essays* (New York: Pantheon, 2001), p. 409.

7. Philip Larkin, "Love Again," in Larkin, *Collected Poems,* ed. Anthony Thwaite (New York: Farrar Straus Giroux, 1989), p. 215.

8. Proust, *The Fugitive,* in *Remembrance of Things Past,* vol. 3, p. 568.

9. Ibid., p. 947.

10. This is the insight of Meg Eliot in Angus Wilson's novel *The Middle Age of Mrs. Eliot* (New York: Viking, 1959), p. 282.

11. Henry James, *The Golden Bowl* (New York: Oxford University Press, 1983), pp. 281–283.

12. Stephen Kern, *The Culture of Love: Victorians to Moderns* (Cambridge, Mass.: Harvard University Press, 1992), p. 272.

13. Ibid., p. 265.

14. Sigmund Freud, *Three Essays on the Theory of Sexuality,* in *The Standard Edition of the Complete Psychological Works of Sigmund Freud,* ed. and trans. James E. Strachey (London: Hogarth Press, 1995), vol. 7, pp. 148, 162.

15. Arnold I. Davidson, *The Emergence of Sexuality* (Cambridge, Mass.: Harvard University Press, 2001), p. 92.

16. Freud, *Three Essays,* p. 187.

17. Samuel Beckett, *Molloy; Malone Dies; The Unnamable* (London: Calder and Boyers, 1959), p. 57.

18. Davidson, *The Emergence of Sexuality,* p. 29.

19. Donald Meltzer, *Sexual States of Mind* (Perthshire: Clunie Press, 1973), p. 65.

20. Melanie Klein, *The Writings of Melanie Klein* (New York: Free Press, 1984), vol. 3, pp. 176–235.

21. Crabb, *English Synonyms,* p. 464.

22. Meltzer, *Sexual States of Mind,* p. 92.

23. Klein, *The Writings of Melanie Klein,* vol. 1, pp. 262–289.

24. Philip Larkin, "This Be the Verse," in *Collected Poems,* p. 180.

25. Sigmund Freud, *Five Lectures on Psychoanalysis,* in *Standard Edition,* vol. 11, pp. 9–20.

26. W. B. Yeats, "The Brown Penny," in *The Collected Poems of W. B. Yeats* (New York: Macmillan, 1950), p. 96.

27. R. D. Hinshelwood, *A Dictionary of Kleinian Thought* (Northvale, N.J.: Aronson, 1991), p. 343.

28. See Alasdair MacIntyre, *Dependent Rational Animals: Why Human Beings Need the Virtues* (Chicago: Open Court, 1999).

29. Arnold H. Modell, "A Narcissistic Defence against Affects and the Illusion of Self-Sufficiency," in Andrew P. Morrison,

ed., *Essential Papers on Narcissism* (New York: New York University Press, 1986), pp. 293–307.

30. D. H. Lawrence, *John Thomas and Lady Jane* (Harmondsworth: Penguin Books, 1974), pp. 73–75. *John Thomas and Lady Jane* is the second draft of *Lady Chatterly's Lover.*

31. Sean O'Faolain, *Vive Moi* (Boston: Little, Brown, 1964), p. 374.

6. SENTIMENTALITY AND THE GIFT OF THE SELF

1. Ivan Turgenev, *Fathers and Sons,* trans. Rosemary Edmonds (Harmondsworth: Penguin Books, 1965), pp. 118–119.

2. Aldous Huxley, *Eyeless in Gaza* (Harmondsworth: Penguin Books, 1955), pp. 48–51.

3. Oscar Wilde to Lord Alfred Douglas, January–March 1897, in Merlin Holland and Rupert Hart-Davis, eds., *The Complete Letters of Oscar Wilde* (New York: Henry Holt, 2000), p. 768.

4. Oscar Wilde, *Lady Windermere's Fan,* in *The Works of Oscar Wilde* (London: Collins, 1966), p. 418.

5.   On the Sabbath-day,

        Through the churchyard old and gray,

Over the crisp and yellow leaves I held my rustling way;

And amid the words of mercy, falling on my soul like balms,

'Mid the gorgeous storms of music—in the mellow organ-calms,

'Mid the upward-streaming prayers, and the rich and solemn psalms,

      I stood careless, Barbara.

      My heart was otherwhere,

        While the organ shook the air,

And the priest, with outspread hands, bless'd the people with a prayer;

But when rising to go homeward, with a mild and saintlike shine

Gleam'd a face of airy beauty with its heavenly eyes on mine—

189

Gleam'd and vanish'd in a moment—O that face was surely
    thine

      Out of heaven, Barbara!

      O pallid, pallid face!
      O earnest eyes of grace!
When last I saw thee, dearest, it was in another place.
You came running forth to meet me with my love-gift on your
    wrist:
The flutter of a long white dress, then all was lost in mist—
A purple stain of agony was on the mouth I kiss'd,
      That wild morning, Barbara.

      I search'd, in my despair,
      Sunny noon and midnight air;
I could not drive away the thought that you were lingering
    there.
O many and many a winter night I sat when you were gone,
My worn face buried in my hands, beside the fire alone—
Within the dripping churchyard, the rain plashing on your
    stone,
      You were sleeping, Barbara.

      'Mong angels, do you think
      Of the precious golden link
I clasp'd around your happy arm while sitting by yon brink?
Or when that night of gliding dance, of laughter and guitars,
Was emptied of its music, and we watch'd, through lattice-bars,
The silent midnight heaven creeping o'er us with its stars,
      Till the day broke, Barbara?

      In the years I've changed;
      Wild and far my heart has ranged,
And many sins and errors now have been on me avenged;
But to you I have been faithful whatsoever good I lack'd:

I loved you, and above my life still hangs that love intact—
Your love the trembling rainbow, I the reckless cataract.

> Still I love you. Barbara.

> Yet, Love, I am unblest;
> With many doubts opprest,

I wander like the desert wind without a place of rest.
Could I but win you for an hour from off that starry shore,
The hunger of my soul were still'd; for Death hath told you
   more
Than the melancholy world doth know—things deeper than all
   lore

> You could teach me, Barbara.

> In vain, in vain, in vain!
> You will never come again.

There droops upon the dreary hills a mournful fringe of rain;
The gloaming closes slowly round, loud winds are in the tree,
Round selfish shores for ever moans the hurt and wounded sea;
There is no rest upon the earth, peace is with Death and thee—

> Barbara!

6. F. R. Leavis, *The Living Principle: English as a Discipline of Thought* (New York: Oxford University Press, 1975), p. 125.

7. Milan Kundera, *The Unbearable Lightness of Being,* trans. Michael Henry Heim (New York: Harper and Row, 1984), pp. 250–251.

8. Lionel Trilling, *Sincerity and Authenticity* (Cambridge, Mass.: Harvard University Press, 1971), p. 104.

9. F. R. Leavis, "Thought and Emotional Quality," in F. R. and Q. D. Leavis, eds., *A Selection from Scrutiny,* vol. 1 (Cambridge: Cambridge University Press, 1968), p. 231.

10. William Blake, "The Marriage of Heaven and Hell: Proverbs

of Hell," in Blake, *The Complete Poems* (Harmondsworth: Penguin Books, 1977), p. 183.

7. LEBENSRAUM, DESIRE, AND THE ENVY OF ETERNITY

1. Eve Kosofsky Sedgwick, *A Dialogue on Love* (New York: Beacon Press, 1999), pp. 24–25.

2. Plato, *Symposium,* trans. Alexander Nehamas and Paul Woodruff, in John M. Cooper, ed., *Plato: Complete Works* (Indianapolis: Hackett, 1989), 177d8–9.

3. Plato, *Lysis,* trans. Stanley Lombardo, in *Plato: Complete Works,* 205e2–206a4.

4. Ibid., 206c4–6.

5. Ibid., 218a2–b1.

6. Plato, *Symposium,* 206e5.

7. Ibid., 208e1–209a4, 209b8, 210a8.

8. Ibid., 209a6–7, 210c1–3.

9. Plato, *Laws,* trans. Trevor Saunders, in *Plato: Complete Works,* 817b1–5.

10. Plato, *Symposium,* 210d5–6.

11. Ibid., 211d3–5.

12. Ibid., 210b4–6.

13. Ibid., 210c5–6.

14. Ibid., 211d8–212a7.

15. Albert O. Hirschman, *Shifting Involvements: Private Interest and Public Action* (Princeton: Princeton University Press, 1982), p. viii.

16. Plato, *Republic,* trans. C. D. C. Reeve (Indianapolis: Hackett, 2004), 585d11–e4.

17. Octavio Paz, *The Double Flame: Love and Eroticism,* trans. Helen Lane (New York: Harcourt Brace, 1995), p. 154.

18. Jacques Lacan, *The Seminar of Jacques Lacan,* Book 2: *The Ego in Freud's Theory and in the Technique of Psychoanalysis, 1954–1955,*

ed. Jacques-Alain Miller, trans. Sylvana Tomaselli (New York: Norton, 1988), p. 223.

19. Ibid., pp. 228–229.

20. See Aristotle, *Nicomachean Ethics,* 10.1–5; idem, *Metaphysics,* Book Lambda, 7–10.

21. William Shakespeare, *Anthony and Cleopatra,* II.ii.243–244.

22. Marcel Proust, *Within a Budding Grove,* in *Remembrance of Things Past,* trans. C. K. Scott Moncrieff, Terence Kilmartin, and Andreas Mayor (New York: Random House, 1981), vol. 1, p. 859.

23. Richard Wollheim, *On the Emotions* (New Haven: Yale University Press, 1999), p. 24.

24. J. G. Ballard, *Cocaine Nights* (Washington, D.C.: Counterpoint, 1998), p. 180.

25. John Keats, "Letter to George and Georgiana Keats, 14, 19 February, ?3, 12, 13, 17, 19 March, 15, 16, 21, 30 April, 3 May 1819," in Elizabeth Cook, ed., *John Keats: The Major Works* (Oxford: Oxford University Press, 1990), pp. 473–474.

26. Mark A. Bedau, "The Nature of Life," in Margaret A. Boden, ed., *The Philosophy of Artificial Life* (Oxford: Oxford University Press, 1996), pp. 332–357.

27. Wallace Stevens, "Esthétique du Mal," in *The Collected Poems of Wallace Stevens* (London: Faber and Faber, 1955), p. 325.

28. Cornelius Castoriadis, *The Imaginary Institution of Society,* trans. Kathleen Blamey (Cambridge, Mass.: MIT Press, 1987), p. 94.

29. Charles Baudelaire, "Recueillement," in Baudelaire, *The Flowers of Evil,* ed. James McGowan (New York: Oxford University Press, 1993), p. 346. My translation.

30. Miguel de Unamuno, *The Tragic Sense of Life* (London: Fontana, 1962), p. 60.

31. Bernard Williams, "The Makropulos Case," in Williams, *Problems of the Self* (Cambridge: Cambridge University Press, 1973), p. 99, note 18.

8. VIOLENCE, PORNOGRAPHY, AND SADOMASOCHISM

1. Carol Gilligan, *The Birth of Pleasure* (New York: Knopf, 2002), p. 160.

2. Ibid., p. 159.

3. Ibid., p. 74.

4. Ibid., p. 143.

5. Ibid., p. 144.

6. Ibid., p. 166.

7. Ibid., p. 162.

8. Alasdair MacIntyre, *After Virtue* (Notre Dame: University of Notre Dame Press, 1981), p. 203.

9. Gilligan, *The Birth of Pleasure,* p. 20.

10. T. Walter Herbert, *Sexual Violence and American Manhood* (Cambridge, Mass.: Harvard University Press, 2002), p. 4.

11. Ibid., p. 5.

12. Ibid., p. 40.

13. Terrence Real, *I Don't Want to Talk about It: Overcoming the Secret Legacy of Male Depression* (New York: Scribner, 1997).

14. Herbert, *Sexual Violence,* pp. 41–42.

15. Ibid., pp. 5–6.

16. Ibid., pp. 53–54.

17. Ibid., pp. 102–103.

18. Ibid., p. 198.

19. Sally Tisdale, *Talk Dirty to Me: An Intimate Philosophy of Sex* (New York: Doubleday, 1994), pp. 139–140.

20. Linda Williams, *Hard Core: Power, Pleasure, and the "Frenzy of the Visible"* (Berkeley: University of California Press, 1989),

p. 273. The reference is to Steven Marcus, *The Other Victorians: A Study of Sexuality and Pornography in Mid-Nineteenth Century England* (New York: New American Library, 1974), p. xiv.

21. Lawrence Kramer, *After the Lovedeath: Sexual Violence and the Making of Culture* (Berkeley: University of California Press, 1997), p. 132.

22. Herbert, *Sexual Violence,* p. 147.

23. Norman Mailer, "The White Negro," *Advertisements for Myself* (New York: Putnam, 1959), p. 339.

24. Chris Hedges, *War Is a Force That Gives Us Meaning* (New York: Public Affairs, 2002), p. 86.

25. Herbert, *Sexual Violence,* pp. 52, 80. The quoted phrase is from David Lisak, "Male Gender Socialization and the Perpetuation of Sexual Abuse," in Ronald F. Levant and William S. Pollack, eds., *A New Psychology of Men* (New York: Basic Books, 1995), p. 161.

26. Plato, *Republic,* trans. C. D. C. Reeve (Indianapolis: Hackett, 2004), 375c6–8.

27. Aristotle, *Ars Rhetorica* (Oxford: Clarendon Press, 1959), 1378a30–2. My translation.

28. Aristotle, *Politics,* trans. C. D. C. Reeve (Indianapolis: Hackett, 1998), 1328a1–3.

29. Homer, *Iliad,* trans. Stanley Lombardo (Indianapolis: Hackett, 1997), pp. 307–308 (Book 16, lines 80–90).

30. Ibid., pp. 358 (Book 18, lines 98–115).

31. Immanuel Kant, *Critique of Judgment,* trans. Paul Guyer and Eric Matthews (Cambridge: Cambridge University Press, 2000), p. 134.

32. Homer, *Iliad,* p. 66 (Book 4, lines 31–37).

33. Deuteronomy 20:10–18; Joshua 6–7, 10:11–14, 28–42, 11:10–15; Matthew 5:22, 25:31–46.

34. Homer, *Iliad,* p. 433 (Book 22, lines 345–347).

35. Homer, *Iliad,* trans. Richmond Lattimore (Chicago: University of Chicago Press, 1951), Book 24, lines 505–506.

36. Homer, *Iliad,* trans. Lombardo, pp. 484–485 (Book 24, lines 560–570). I have substituted "anger" for Lombardo's "grief" as a translation of *thumos* in line 568.

37. Simone Weil, "The *Iliad,* Poem of Might," in George A. Panichas, ed., *The Simone Weil Reader* (New York: McKay, 1981), p. 153.

38. Susan Sontag, *Regarding the Pain of Others* (New York: Farrar Straus Giroux, 2003), p. 12.

39. Christopher Logue, *War Music: An Account of Books 16–19 of Homer's Iliad* (London: Jonathan Cape, 1981), p. 72.

40. Octavio Paz, *An Erotic Beyond: Sade,* trans. Elliot Weinberger (New York: Harcourt Brace, 1998), p. 73.

41. Michel Foucault, "Sex, Power and the Politics of Identity," in Sylvère Lotringer, ed., *Foucault Live* (New York: Semiotext(e), 1989), p. 384.

42. Ibid., p. 384.

43. Ibid., p. 382.

44. Mark Edmundson, *Nightmare on Main Street: Angels, Sadomasochism, and the Culture of Gothic* (Cambridge, Mass.: Harvard University Press), pp. 130–131.

45. Ibid., p. 135.

46. Ibid., p. 131.

47. Ibid., pp. 142–143.

9. WORK AND/AS LOVE

1. Homer, *Odyssey,* trans. Stanley Lombardo (Indianapolis: Hackett, 2000), 174 (Book 11, line 540).

2. Ibid., pp. 138–139 (Book 9, lines 502–505).

3. Ibid., p. 125 (Book 9, lines 5–11).

4. Plato, *Republic,* trans. C. D. C. Reeve (Indianapolis: Hackett, 2004), 390a8–b4.

5. Homer, *Odyssey,* p. 125 (Book 9, lines 19–20).

6. Ibid., p. 7 (Book 1, lines 214–216).

7. Ibid., p. 18 (Book 2, lines 116–121).

8. Alfred Heubeck, Stephanie West, and J. B. Hainsworth, eds., *A Companion to Homer's Odyssey,* vol. 1 (Oxford: Oxford University Press, 1988), p. 139.

9. Laurent Cantet, *Time Out* (France: ThinkFilm, Inc., 2001).

10. Richard Sennett, *The Corrosion of Character: The Personal Consequences of Work in the New Capitalism* (New York: Norton, 1988), p. 15.

11. Ibid., pp. 15–16.

12. Ibid., p. 22.

13. Ibid., p. 31.

14. Ibid., pp. 22–23.

15. Ibid., p. 26.

16. Ibid., p. 148.

17. Ibid., pp. 62–63.

18. Ibid., p. 147.

19. Ludwig Wittgenstein, MS 107 176 c: 24.10.1929, in *Wittgenstein's Nachlass: The Bergen Electronic Edition* (Oxford: Oxford University Press, 2000). This CD-ROM contains the complete philosophical writings as catalogued in G. H. von Wright, ed., *The Wittgenstein Papers* (1982).

20. Svetlana Boym, *The Future of Nostalgia* (New York: Basic Books, 2001), pp. 41–48.

21. V. S. Naipaul, *The Return of Eva Perón* (New York: Knopf, 1980), p. 204. "Authenticity" is Naipaul's term for restorative nostalgia.

22. Eva Ilouz, *Consuming: Love and the Cultural Contradictions of*

Capitalism (Berkeley: University of California Press, 1997), p. 290.

23. Ibid., p. 293.

24. Richard Wollheim, "The Sheep and the Ceremony," in Wollheim, *The Mind and Its Depths* (Cambridge, Mass.: Harvard University Press, 1993), p. 9.

25. Georg Christoph Lichtenberg, *The Waste Books,* trans. R. J. Hollingdale (New York: New York Review Books, 2000), p. 71.

26. Oscar Wilde, *De Profundis,* in *The Works of Oscar Wilde* (London: Collins, 1966), p. 920.

10. SEX, DEMOCRACY, AND THE FUTURE OF LOVE

1. Gérard Vincent, "A History of Secrets?" in Philippe Ariès and George Duby, eds., *A History of Private Life,* vol. 5: *Riddles of Identity in Modern Times,* ed. Antoine Prost and Gérard Vincent, trans. Arthur Goldhammer (Cambridge, Mass.: Harvard University Press, 1991), pp. 269, 272.

2. Elizabeth Benedict, *The Joy of Writing Sex: A Guide for Fiction Writers* (New York: Owl Books and Henry Holt, 2002), p. 23.

3. Susan Morrison, "The Wit and Fury of Martin Amis," *Rolling Stone* (May 17, 1990), pp. 101–102.

4. Lynn Jamieson, *Intimacy: Personal Relationships in Modern Societies* (Oxford: Polity Press, 1998), p. 158.

5. Anthony Giddens, *The Transformation of Intimacy: Sexuality, Love, and Eroticism in Modern Societies* (Stanford: Stanford University Press, 1992), pp. 2, 199.

6. Ibid., p. 147.

7. Lawrence Kramer, *After the Lovedeath: Sexual Violence and the Making of Culture* (Berkeley: University of California Press, 1997), p. 12.

8. Giddens, *The Transformation of Intimacy,* p. 94.

9. Ibid., p. 144.

10. Ibid., pp. 202, 95.

11. Adam Phillips, *Monogamy* (New York: Pantheon, 1996), preface.

12. Octavio Paz, *An Erotic Beyond: Sade,* trans. Elliot Weinberger (New York: Harcourt Brace, 1998), p. 69.

13. Jamieson, *Intimacy,* p. 174.

14. Lord Byron, *Beppo* (1818), Canto I, stanza 194.

15. Leo Bersani, *The Freudian Body: Psychoanalysis and Art* (New York, 1986), pp. 39–40.

16. Candace Vogler, "Sex and Talk," in Lauren Berlant, ed., *Intimacy* (Chicago: University of Chicago Press, 2000), p. 76.

17. Simon Blackburn, *Lust* (New York: Oxford University Press, 2004), p. 100.

18. Tracey Fox, "He's Mr. Right—For Now," *The Sunday Times* [London] (June 15, 2003), Style Section, p. 24.

19. Tibor Scitovsky, *The Joyless Economy* (New York: Oxford University Press, 1992), p. viii.

20. David Archard, "Sex Education," in Randall Curren, ed., *A Companion to the Philosophy of Education* (Oxford: Blackwell, 2003), p. 543.

21. Phillips, *Monogamy,* p. 38.

22. Mavis Gallant, *The Affair of Gabrielle Russier* (New York; Knopf, 1971), p. 15.

ACKNOWLEDGMENTS

My thoughts about love initially took shape in a seminar ("The Love Class," as it came to be called) at Reed College, and were subsequently developed in one at Chapel Hill. Steve Arkonovich, Neera Badhwar, Anne Baker, Dorit Bar-On, Lucia Binotti, Jenann Ismael, Rachel Kratz, and Patrick Miller discussed early versions, criticizing and inspiring. Anne, in particular, confused me as much about love as I her—more, probably. Eight anonymous readers introduced me to work I didn't know, detected errors I hadn't noticed, helped me to see what I had written in a new light, and—in one instance—advised me not to publish this book under my own name! I wish I could thank each of them more personally. By sheer chance, I can now at least thank one of them. So, thank you Candace Vogler—for writing a very personal assessment of the manuscript. Paul Woodruff was never anonymous, because he identified himself as my friend. He was and is that in spades.

In response to an email, Janet Zweig received some ancestor

or other of this book. One thing led to another, as things have a tendency to do, with the result that her ideas about love became an important influence on me. For emailing and all the other -ings, I am in her debt.

Conversations over dinner at Panzanella with Ram Neta represented intellectual collegiality at its best. His subsequent written comments, responding to almost every page, were further proof of his generosity and insightfulness. My longtime editor at Hackett Publishing Company, Deborah Wilkes, was the first reader of each of many versions (one a dialogue for four characters!). Without her faith and encouragement, *Love's Confusions* wouldn't exist. At Harvard University Press, Maria Ascher and Lindsay Waters provided editorial support of the very highest order—Lindsay's long phone conversations, in particular, led me to read new books, listen to new music, and think new thoughts. I am deeply grateful to them both.

Finally, I thank two wonderful analysts, Duane Dale and Julia Danek.

INDEX